CLASSROOM MANAGEME[N]

DAYS:

The Most Effective Classroom Management Method for Middle and High School Teachers

Find Out the Classroom Management Secrets, Tips & Tricks

Mohamed A. Ansary

Five Star Faculty Award Finalist

The University of Arizona

mansary@email.arizona.edu

Selected Amazon Reviews: Classroom: Classroom Management in Five Days: The Most Effective Classroom Management Method for Teachers: Find Out the Classroom Management Secrets, Tips & Tricks Paperback – October 25, 2018

by Mohamed A. Ansary (Author)
https://amzn.to/2Pi6h7P

I loved reading this book because as a first-year classroom teacher, I'm inundated with resources for classroom management and oftentimes OVERWHELMED by the amount of material and techniques out there. Ansary offers a clear, comprehensive and concise picture of classroom management. He touches on all aspect from lesson design to daily structure to anxiety and anger among students.

Ansary clearly understands the importance of treating the student's social and emotional needs before their academic. I especially appreciated his section on alleviating student anxiety as it relates directly to several of my 2nd graders. Thank you, Mohamed Ansary, for this wonderful resource! I marked it up and will put it in my teaching library!

I enjoyed reading this book. The format was laid out for an easy read with a common-sense approach of hints and advice for managing a classroom. Great ideas for teachers of all areas to making the classroom a community for fun and learning.

If you buy one book on the topic of classroom management, make it this one. The classes that we've taken on teaching methods and management certainly have their place, but there's no replacement for the breadth of experience that Dr. Ansary brings to the table.

Ansary has taught students of all levels in multiple countries and across multiple subjects; he's identified those classroom management techniques which apply universally and successfully. The methods he describes here are tested and proven by his own years of experience. Anything short of that was omitted from the book.

As many of us have learned, there's an enormous difference between teaching theory and teaching practice. Dr. Ansary learned this a long time ago and has given you the classroom management skills which took him years to develop and fully understand.

Don't take years to learn what Ansary can teach you today. Save yourself the time (and yes, the frustration) and buy this book instead.

Great book for beginner and veteran teachers alike. If you're first stepping foot into the teaching world or are trying to figure out how to manage your classroom most effectively, this book is definitely for you. The writing is easy and accessible, and it gets straight to the point. Ansary knows how to work the classroom to the greatest benefit - and teaches us how to do the same!

This will show you wonderful teaching methods. In this book, you will find hints and tips on classroom management. I'd recommend this book to any professor/teacher looking for assistance controlling their students.

This is a collection of guidelines for creating and maintaining a healthy classroom environment. It is uncluttered and easy to read for an objective assessment of current practices or criteria to keep in mind in class development. Good overview of all aspects of classroom management.

One more good book from Dr. Ansary! Briefly, but very productively, he touches up the issues that most of educator's face, and proposes practical solutions, combining modern and classical pedagogical approaches. SRONGLY RECOMMEND!

As a teacher it has been hard to find creative ways to engage my students, this book has great tools for maintaining my students' attention and comprehension.

Classroom Technology: How to Use Technology in the Classroom: (2018 Classroom
Technology Guide with tips and tricks) Top Tech Tools for K-16 Teachers and ...
Technology in your Classroom Book 1) Kindle Edition
by Mohamed A. Ansary (Author)
https://amzn.to/2PjNk4T

As a student with experience in many of the programs and methods described in
Ansary's book, I can say from first-hand experience that not only do these
recommendations and methods work, but they allow both students and teachers to
experience language instruction in new ways. Ansary's experience in language
instruction combine with his genuine love for technology to produce a guide that is as
readable as it is applicable; he expertly explains the what, why and how of each
recommendation in his book.

Programs like EdPuzzle (one example of many mentioned in the book) provide
students a new and relatable way to study their target languages, and it only makes
sense that they (we) gain so quickly in classrooms which incorporate technology in
their methods: we are the least likely generation in history to leave home without
technology within immediate reach. From smart phones to smart watches to in-dash
touch screens and beyond, we have grown accustomed to (and come to expect)
integrated technology in our day-to-day endeavors. Ansary understands this concept
and harnesses available language-learning technology to the advantage of both
students and instructors.

I can't recommend this book enough for language instructors looking for proven,
technological methods of innovating in the classroom, and there is no better source
than Dr. Mohamed Ansary.

I have been learning two languages for several years now, and my only regret is that
all my professors over the years haven't read this book. As an aspiring professor
myself, I found this book to be extremely informative. With the technology advances
of today, we need to learn how to use our advantages to the best of our abilities, and
Ansary outlines exactly how to do that. A must read for not only language instructors
but ALL instructors who want to take advantage of the technology of today.

From all The Informational Ocean of Technology for the Classroom, Dr. Ansary
through his own expertise has selected several the most beneficial technologies for the
modern classroom, which MUST have at least some of them. He does not overload
non-experts (at least, I speak of myself) with lectures about modern technologies, but
simply and effectively explains, how to practically use these technologies, and the
benefits for using them.
In addition to a good help, this book turns modern educators towards many interesting
aspects of HOW a language (and not only) might be ALSO taught and students'
knowledge ALSO be checked, enables both of them developing their further
creativity, and opens new perspectives in what might seem already travail aspects of
teaching and learning.

I have been learning two languages for several years now, and my only regret is that all my professors over the years haven't read this book. As an aspiring professor myself, I found this book to be extremely informative. With the technology advances of today, we need to learn how to use our advantages to the best of our abilities, and Ansary outlines exactly how to do that. A must read for not only language instructors but ALL instructors who want to take advantage of the technology of today.

Meditation: Meditation for Beginners: A 20 Day How to Meditate Program: Inner Peace, Stress Relief, Mental Health & Mindfulness Ultra Effective Meditation and Mindfulness Guide Kindle Edition

By Mohamed A. Ansary (Author), Helen Ruth Clifford (Author)
https://amzn.to/2PgpruZ

If you just can't manage to clear your mind enough to meditate, this book is for you, as it'll give you great (and easy to adapt to) guidelines on how to get to the mindfulness that we all want to achieve. Ansary does a great job of taking the reader through several steps to meditation without ever making the reader feel lost or confused.

Absolutely loved this book and could not stop reading until I finished it! Dr. Ansary moves his readers through the extremely simple and at the same time efficient steps. Following them will be paid off, starting from the very first days of our over busy and overstressed life.

In the past, I have tried various different books to mediate. This one has been one of the best since it very clear and precise. Being clear is very important when trying to teach beginners on how to meditate properly. This book really allowed me to clear my conscience. It also helped me have a clear mind throughout the day. :)

How many among us need a book like this in such a brisk life, where we do not have the time even to entertain ourselves and soothe our spirits.

FREE

GRAB YOUR COPY
THE UNCONVENTIONAL GUIDE TO CLASSROOM
ASSESSMENT   "CHAPTER ONE"

Mohamed A. Ansary

MOHAMED ANSARY

MANSARY@EMAIL.ARIZOAN.EDU

CLASSROOM ASSESSMENT

FIVE STAR FACULTY AWARD
FINALIST, 2018

Find Out the
Classroom
Assessment Secrets.

Principles and
Practices

FREE COPY

MOHAMED A. ANSARY

TIPS AND TRICKS

Table of Contents

Introduction

I want to thank you and congratulate you for purchasing the book,

Classroom Management in Five Days.

This book contains proven steps and strategies on how to manage your classroom effectively. You will learn how to:

- Make your classroom into a happy, fun, inspirational learning environment that will motivate and inspire your students.

- Minimize the incidence of bad behavior and know how to address it simply and effectively.

No more will you have spitballs flying above your head. No more will you have students making so much noise that you cannot be heard.

Poor classroom management is a principal cause of excess stress on teachers that can lead to poor academic success from students and a high burnout rate for teachers.

Teachers, this is not another text book to weigh you down with steps, procedures, methods, strategies, etc. You have already read all that, done all that, and got the t-shirt for it. You have passed with flying colors all tests. It is time for you to enjoy.

This book is dedicated to the honorable, highly qualified professional that you are.

Most teachers face one of the biggest challenges of securing a focused classroom; one that is free of distractions.

This book takes you through the actions you can use in a classroom that not only gain the attention of the children, but also help them to succeed while being taught by you. In an environment of learning, you are never taught to expect the kind of disruption you may be subjected to and all of the information in this book is based on vast experience in the classroom in a number of schools with kids of different disruptive levels. Some of these kids believe they will never learn. Some of them think they are too clever to be forced to be in a classroom. You have to remember that the world out there isn't that easy for kids. We say that the technological age gives them power, but it also means that they have less contact with others, rather than more.

In this book, you will learn how to improve your classroom management skills. This can be done by using straightforward, easy to adapt, techniques that will motivate, inspire and reward your students and reduce the incidence of poor behavior.

πøπSo, if you're ready to develop useful and effective classroom management techniques, let's get started! Thanks again for purchasing this book, I hope you enjoy it!

and brands within this book are for clarifying purposes only and are owned by the owners themselves, not affiliated with this document.

Chapter 1: What is classroom management

Classroom management refers to a process, which makes it possible for teachers and professors to control the direction and learning of a classroom. It is used to develop and maintain the focus of students on learning and at the same time prevent distractions or disruptions from decelerating the process of learning. Teachers use classroom management strategies and techniques such as those focused on cooperation and direction, so that students do not disrupt their peers or become distracted by their peers.

Given that classroom management allows classes to be on track, as well as guarantees the prevention of distractions and disruptions that slow down the process of learning, it is considered as one of the most significant aspects of providing high-quality education.

Teachers, you have Classroom Management skills that you have not even been recognized for. You have been ignored far too long for the skills you possess. Within you lies the power that transforms lives into special vessels of honor. You are the catapult of all great things. You have been taught by the best – yourselves. You have taught yourselves new strategies and techniques when no one else could. Sure, there were countless professional development classes you attended, but none of those presenters knew your students like you. They all presented what they thought were great ideas, but could they implement them in your classroom without you being there to keep order. Many articles and books have been consulted to find out a vivid description of classroom management. The most common definition of classroom management states that it is a practice with a goal of establishing and encouraging the self-control of students through promoting positive student behavior and achievement. In addition, the concept of classroom management is also associated with teacher's effectiveness, teacher-student relationship, and academic achievement. There are three major components of classroom management. These include conduct management, contract management, and content management. Most teachers already know that the high occurrence of classroom problems when it comes to discipline, has a huge negative impact on the efficiency of teaching, as well as learning.

Research shows that teachers who deal with disciplinary problems failed to plan and implement appropriate instructional modules. These teachers may have also neglected to put variety in their lessons and evaluate the materials they use for the conducive learning of the students.

In addition, the comprehension of students is not monitored regularly. Teachers who implement consistent management and use organizational skills have classrooms that experience lesser problems when it comes to discipline.

Principles of Classroom Management

Whether a teacher is a novice or seasoned one, having his or her own classroom comes with a number of responsibilities. These include creating instructional components, learning the school's curriculum, establishing classroom rules, setting goals, and learning policies and procedures.

It is important to take note that any decision that a teacher makes in a particular school year could have consequences on the lives of his or her students, as well as, his or her professional career. One of the most fundamental decisions that teachers make, focuses on how they are able to manage their classroom. This decision centers on the creation and maintenance of a specific learning atmosphere.

In making decisions, teachers should bear in mind some of the basic principles of classroom management, which are applicable to all teaching styles and grade levels.

Teaching Styles and Preferences

More often than not, teachers apply management styles, regardless if they fit their teaching preferences. It is important for teachers to assess their expectations from their students, especially their behavior during class. Teachers should have a clear view of how they want a particular school day to work once the students arrive and leave the classroom.

For instance, teachers should discern if they want their students to work quietly in their seats or provide a number of activities. Even small actions in the classroom are necessary for a successful classroom management system. Thus, teachers should discern if they would permit the students to sharpen their pencils as needed or only at a specified period. Teachers should also contemplate if they want their students to raise their hands or approach their desks if they have questions. These are simple actions that affect classroom management; thus, teachers should discern the rules that they deem best for their personal teaching styles, preferences, and tolerances.

Keeping a Simple Classroom Management System

Once the teachers are able to identify their teaching styles and preferences to have order in the classroom, it would be easy to develop or adopt a classroom Proven Classroom Management Strategies management system. The basis for a classroom management system is the rules that describe the expectations of teachers to students. The rules only need to be few to make it easier for teachers to enforce them and for students to follow them.

Establishing classroom rules should not only focus on a specific activity in a particular part of the school day. For instance, students may raise their hand if they want to speak. This is a rule that is applicable for the entire instructional day. On the other hand, it is better to establish a rule, which is more specific such as "respect your neighbors." This implicates that students should not interrupt their teachers or classmates at any time.

Integrating Positive Reinforcement

When refining a classroom management system, it is necessary for teachers to contemplate on the reason for having school rules; that is, to teach and develop acceptable behavior. Once teachers create their rules based on this reason, they may establish powerful classroom rules with positive behaviors. For instance, instead of having a rule of "raise your hand and wait for you to be called," teachers may create a rule that says, "Do not speak while others are not done speaking."

Rules that are phrased positively, make way for teachers to teach, develop, and reinforce positive behavior while maintaining order in the classroom.

Developing, practicing, teaching, modelling, or reinforcing rules should be based on appropriate behavior instead of merely catching students who behave inappropriately. In addition, it is also advisable to reward the students who follow the rules and engage in positive and appropriate behaviors.

Making Simple, Gradual Changes

Not all classroom management systems run in seamless flow as much as not all students follow the rules effortlessly. In fact, teachers are likely to discipline the same students again and again. For instance, a teacher may find out that she has not spoken with student A for an entire school week even if such student comes to class daily with his homework and never gives trouble. In this case, the teacher should make simple, yet gradual changes to her classroom management system.

When making changes in a classroom management system, it is important to establish small ones rather than implementing huge changes at once. Teachers would only find it more taxing to make large changes, which might also confuse the students. It would be helpful if a teacher asks a colleague to observe his or her classroom management system for feedback. The feedback could provide the teacher necessary information with respect to the changes he or she needs to make.

Starting from Day One

One of the most common mistakes that teachers make is giving their students a "training" or "adjustment" period in which they are not held accountable yet for any rules violated in the classroom, Proven Classroom Management Strategies simply because they are still learning or adjusting. However, students should be able to learn the expectations of their teachers, by being held accountable for their behavior from Day One. Teachers need to enforce the classroom rules from the very first time they get in the classroom. This implies a message that the rules of the teachers are important and should be enforced and followed.

Rules should be taught, practiced, modelled, and regularly reviewed at the start of the school year, as well as periodically. Choosing a Classroom Management System Teachers are able to determine if they are implementing effective classroom management if they see the difference between a classroom where students struggle to attain educational objectives and a classroom where students are attentive and focused. In general, teachers find it difficult to choose the most suitable classroom management system. However, depending on their teaching styles and preferences, teachers may choose whether to implement a classroom management system that centers on establishing a collaborative relationship with students or a direct approach to lead and manage their classrooms.

Advantages of Classroom Management

In order to ensure that students learn in an environment free of distraction and disruption, effective classroom management is enormously necessary. Having an effective classroom management is significant in ensuring that students are able to achieve their full academic capabilities. Students develop, maintain, improve, and/or enhance academic results if teachers are able to control the behavior and direction of a classroom effectively. Thus, a good classroom management system is advantageous for both teachers and students. Moreover, high-quality classroom management allows teachers to prevent students from being distracted or causing disruptions to the peers, which may set back their learning potentials. There are several challenges that teachers face when it comes to classroom management. These include, disruptive students; who interrupt or slow down the learning pace, and ineffective management strategies that aggravate the behavior of students. Effective teachers usually know a variety of effective classroom management strategies and implement appropriate measures to maintain a class focused on achieving educational objectives and free of disruption. The difference between a classroom that is behind the average and a focused classroom that reaches its educational objectives often determines the efficiency of classroom management. It is important for teachers to have an adequate understanding of classroom management, as well as the ability to implement strategies to keep their classroom focused on achieving its academic productivity and objectives. In this book, both new and seasoned teachers would be able to learn classroom management strategies, which could be implemented throughout the school year. This book is divided into three parts. Part one discusses classroom management strategies for the beginning of the school year. Part two discusses midyear classroom management strategies. Finally, Part three discusses classroom management strategies for the end of the school year.

Chapter 2: Know Who You Are

Most noble of professions is that of Teacher. We know that identity in all things is critical. However, it is most serious in the teaching profession. Knowing who you are requires a few introspective questions.

- Why am I in this profession?
- What is important in this profession?
- How do I share knowledge?

From these three questions, you can arrive at the 'heart' of the answers.

The reason this book is entitled "Simplicity of Classroom Management" is because all you need to know comes from within you, the Teacher. This is not a text manual for you to study the techniques of teaching. Any type of successful strategy must be intrinsic.

Being an authority, and knowing the same intrinsically, totally obliterates any problem of classroom management. This knowledge is definitely communicated to students without you ever saying a word.

To have the capacity to give knowledge is a profound concept. When we share knowledge, we are saying, "I care about you. I want the highest and best for you. I want you to go beyond your reach." As students observe this, they can sense the authority along with the love. When their hearts are at peace, they don't feel a need to challenge you.

Whether you know this on the surface or not, love is what you stand for. That is what teaching is about. You as a Teacher are the epitome of love. Never forget that. Students are good observers. They watch very closely what we say, and most of all what we do.

Knowing who you are is so very important to the teaching profession. Why? Because students will know. If there is an uncertainty in you, students will pick up on it. If they don't catch your discomfort immediately, they have several ways to spot it.

Now, don't let their little ways of testing you trip you up. Acting out here and there is only a test. Such behaviors are not personal. Always know that, so then you won't forget why you are there. One point of information is to know that students are searching for identity.

Don't take 'acting out' personally because on the surface students are not aware of the whys for their behavior. Our students are looking for the authority figure to create structure. Know who you are and why you are in the profession. Simple, right? Right! When society complicates things, that is when trouble starts. Institutions want to analyze the world to the state of non-effect. It is the tradition of man that has tried to make the law of God of no effect. Therefore, we see the chaos and malfeasance that is not only in our schools, but in the world at large.

You see, as we are first faithful to ourselves in knowing who we are and why we are in the profession, this naturally translates to the students. This translates effectively because students see the real you. They see the love in your demeanor, and the stance you take on important issues. Students see that teaching them is very important to you.

They see it by your interactions with them – and with others concerning them. What students observe in you makes them reverence and appreciate you. These students feel a love emanating from you they will never forget.

Your Reputation Will Perceive You

Whether teachers want a reputation or not they will have one. The reputation you create will last as long as you want it to last. A teacher will have a reputation with your co-teachers, and you will have one with your students. If you recall when you were a student in school, you knew your teacher's reputation before you even went into the classroom.

If teachers are seasoned, they can still gain control their classroom. Just as the word got out that your class is a joke. This can also change when you implement these new systems. This book will discuss how to have your students hating you today and how they will love you tomorrow. Think back to when you were a student. Remember the teachers where you did not have to do any work and come to class and play? Then when you when to college and realized how much you were behind, you hated those teachers. You love those teachers with high expectations and hate those who did not. These were the teachers who taught you discipline, and you actually learned. These teachers were the rulers of their classroom. You can do the same and rule your kingdom.

Chapter 3: Pre-Planning

Preplanning is usually a week before the students actually return to school. It is five days where teachers can plan their classrooms so they can be prepared for work when the students return. If a teacher has not experienced preplanning, it can be overwhelming.

Teachers will quickly find out that being in college is a lot easier than being in the workforce. Teacher will have to get fingerprints, get a password to get on the computer, attend faculty meetings, attend departmental meetings, go to the District office, **etc.**

The teacher's union will be trying to get you to join. I hope the teacher is not a coach? Teachers will have to go to football practice which takes away from getting the classroom ready.

This is just a few of the things that a new teacher will have to do all and the teacher has not even touched the classroom yet. It even gets worse if the teacher has to move from out of town. There are many things that will need to be done there. Teachers are trying to get their utilities and cable turned on and at the same time gets their children registered for school.

Teachers have to do stuff for the principal. Teachers have to attend a meeting with the assistant principal that deals with discipline and/or attendance. Staff will have to decide whether or not teachers are going to do morning or evening duty. Teacher must decorate their classroom. How will the teacher arrange his or her class? This is just crazy, what do you do? There is a lot going on?

Instead of preparing for the classroom, teachers do all these other things which will have a direct impact on classroom management. I suggest doing none of these things unless a deadline is given and prepare the classroom. The classroom is more important. Getting information back to the office will not help a teacher manage his or her class. Teachers need to set it up early so they can be prepared for the students.

Ask to begin working on your classroom a week before preplanning starts. School will be open so this will not be a problem.

Is your classroom clean?

Before the topic of how to arrange a classroom is touched, be sure the classroom is clean. A clean environment is important for classroom management. Clean every ounce of your classroom from top to bottom. Wipe down every desk, chair, board **etc.**

Is there anything hanging from the ceiling? Take out those staplers from the wall and clean that bookshelf. If you are new teacher, you will probably have the worse classroom on campus. Teachers who are returning have traded up to a better class and will give the worse class on campus. Become friends with the custodian and ask for cleaning supplies. Ask to replace anything that is unclean and spray air freshener to eliminate the foul odor. Clean those windows and wipe those blinds down.

Work to maintain a clean classroom daily. If students write on the desks or wall, clean it up quickly. This can turn into classroom behavior issues when another student writes about another student.

How to arrange your Classroom Door?

Believe it or not the door not the classroom sets the tone. Your door should have your Name, Subject(s) and the name of all the students in your classroom by period clearly labeled and defined on the outside of your door. It should have your complete schedule along with the time, homeroom, lunch, and even your planning period.

Decorations are OK with elementary school but should be limited with middle and high school. When student see all the decorations on the door; it gives the perception of a fun class which means a class to play in. Set the tone that your class is about business.

The main reason why teachers should want this on the door an in large enough font is because teachers do not want students to enter the class who should not be in the class. New students will open the door and ask what class this is, and this could cause disruption which could begin the start of classroom disruption from the first day of school.

Place a schedule of your classes on the door where students can clearly read it without them disrupting your class. Be sure to include homeroom, duty, lunch **etc.** Update the schedule when new students are added. If a student comes in and asks a question, instruct them to have a seat and move them onwards quickly. Stay ready for your class this is crucial especially on day one.

How to decorate the classroom?

Ineffective teachers decorate the classroom. Effective teachers allow his or her students to decorate the classroom. As I mentioned earlier, teacher is the ruler. Does the king do the work or the servants? Teachers must get in their mind set to get students to do as much as they can. Besides teachers already know how to do it, even better, the students want to do it. Besides, light classroom decorations, have the students to decorate the room.

During preplanning the teacher should put construction paper on all of the bulletin boards. The boards should be neatly done to show students the importance of detail and high expectation from day one. A student notice details and have a neatly prepared bulletin board sets the tone. Now, I did not say anything about putting anything on these boards. These boards should be left bare. Maybe just a picture or so until you have the students to put up his or her work. They should not be fully decorated. Yes, the room should be filled with student examples of essays, projects, and assignments. You can begin to put them up after the first month of school. Then you can continue to upgrade the boards as frequent as you can.

This is important because the students are going to decorate these boards with their school work. In fact, if the teacher has a student helper, have them to decorate the board with construction paper. Remember, that your job is to facilitate and to point fingers and have the students to do everything including hanging pictures and work on your wall. Remember, that students often misbehave because they do not have anything to do. After the first two weeks of school, the teacher can have students to put up their work on your boards.

Keep thinking to yourself and begin to ask yourself, can the students do it?

How to arrange the classroom desks?

During your training, teachers will be taught how to use cooperative teaching methods. Cooperative learning has to do with putting students in some form of groups. This is a very effective teaching strategy, but it should not be done at the beginning of school. Students have to be trained on how to participate in group activities. Also, the teacher should know the students more before putting students together. Who had a fight at the end of school last year? Not knowing these things could cause you problems at the beginning of school.

Your class should be set up in the traditional way with classroom rows. Classroom rows are done for the purpose of management and control. It will allow the teacher to see each student in his or her face.

The second important reason why students should be in rows is because of attendance. Most schools require teachers to be standing at the door in between bells. The purpose of teacher putting the students in rows is because you are going to already have the students' name on the desk in alphabetical order. Do not allow students to sit themselves in your class. The students who cause the most trouble are going to sit in the back and will sit beside each other. You, as the teacher will, have problems on the first day of school. Yes, it may be a few where this may happen, but not enough where it will cause a problem.

Now, you can stand at the door and greet your students and you will instruct each student to find his or her name on the desk and have a seat. If a new student comes in that is not on the list, just have that student to sit at the last seat with no name on it or the last row that teacher can set aside. Do not rearrange the seats daily. Once the teacher places the seats for the first day, keep it that way for several weeks. Teachers want to create a routine for the students so that every time the student comes into the classroom he or she will report to the same seat. Keep your kingdom in line.

Teachers will receive a class roll from the assistant principal. If the roll has 27 students on the roll, divide your desks up in rows of five, for example, if teacher has 30 desks. This will give teacher six rows. Keep the rows short if possible so as teacher you can walk in front and in the back of the classroom. This will allow you to monitor the classroom from the front and the back. Do not allow the students to move the desks. Do not allow a student to sit in an unassigned seat. Be vocal and enforce your rules especially at the beginning.

Use index cards and tape the names down on each desk securely. Use as much tape as needed so students will not take the cards off the desk. Do not use post it notes. If possible, laminate the cards so students can not write on them. If students write on the cards replace them immediately. It will save teachers a lot of headache if teacher photocopy all the cards before taping them on the desk.

Do not put your class in groups, place students in rows with their names in alphabetical order on the desks and instruct them to find their names and be seated.

Have supplies for students readily available

If you are one of those teachers who believes that students should bring their own supplies? You are asking for trouble. Why cause yourself trouble? Give it to them. If you want to have better classroom management, than provide supplies to the student. Is it really worth it for your class to get out of control because a student does not bring a book? If a student does not bring a book to class, the student will begin to talk and become disruptive. The same goes if the student does not have paper or pencil.

When giving the reading annotation assignment, the book should be already located under the desk. This allows for less movement as possible. If the teacher put the books in the front of the class and have the students to walk up and grab a book, students will push or hit each other, thus, causing disruption. Place the book under the desk or have the first person from each row to pass out the book for each row. Allow one student to come up at a time. The same goes when books are being put back. The students should be doing everything. The only thing the teacher should be doing is pointing your finger; remember teachers are the king of the classroom.

Calling the Roll

This is mistake number one calling the roll the first day of school. This is why you have assigned seats. Just look for the missing student and you know the student is not present. One mistake teachers make is calling the roll on the first day of school. The reasons why teachers do not want to do this is because if the teacher say a student's name wrong the student will surely let the teacher know and this will immediately open the door for misbehavior.

Students who know the correct pronunciation of the name will begin to laugh and the person whose name you have mispronounced will defend his or her name and will often correct you as rudely enough so other students will laugh at you. So, before class has already started, ineffective teachers have lost control of the class.

This is the reason why students are placed in alphabetical order on desks in rows. Attendance will take only a few seconds because all the teacher has to do is look at the empty seats. Your school will require the teacher to provide body counts of the student who are present or absent. Teachers can get this done in lightning speed.

Please do not play the get to know you games the first day of school. The students will immediately think your class is a joke. They are preparing to take over your kingdom. It should be about business the first day of class. A student will have the nerve to make statements about how they are playing games in the other classes. Talk less, you do not have to explain, you are the king. Point your finger while saying as few words as possible and instruct students to get to work.

What teacher should do while the students are working?

The teacher should be ruling the kingdom what else? The first week of school you should be on your feet walking around the classroom like the king of the jungle. While what a mighty kingdom you are creating. Teacher's objective is to walk and help, but do not allow students to talk much if not at all. Students should not be helping each other out. This is the reason why the work should be something they can do. Teachers are establishing their reputation as a teacher that students come to class to work.

This is why space is needed as much as possible to walk all the way around the classroom. Do not let your students come up for air to breathe. If a student stops work or begin to talk, just ask, "Is there a problem?" Walk toward the student and instruct the student to get back to work. Do not let up! Do not feel sorry, provide no empathy, stay on task and continue to have them to work day in and day out from the time they walk in the classroom until the time they walk out. Especially the first two weeks.

Now while they are working, teacher should slip away to the teacher's desk. You can take the roll. The reason why teacher want to do this is because you will need to complete all of that administrative work. You are not trying to live on campus after school. Spend a few minutes getting your tasks done than walk around in your dictator style, owning your classroom. Than complete your tasks while they are completing theirs. Sit in the front of the class and watch them like a hawk. When they look up, stare them down and they will get back to work.

As you may have already guessed, your desk should be in front of the classroom. Teachers should be able to look at their faces. Do not place the teacher's desk behind their back. This is where most bullying occurs because it happens when the teacher cannot see the students' face. Students can whisper and make noises and distractions and the teacher will not even know who did it. If as all possible have the desk in front of the classroom or facing the side never behind the students.

When to go over your school rules?

Do not go over class rules until you are sure this is the class you will have. This means that the administration has stopped taking kids out and adding kids to your class. The school has settled down. This can take between four and 10 days. In the meanwhile, be sure to have to students work on the assignments until you have decided to go over the rules.

Students must be trained on what to do in your classroom and know the rules of the school. They do not already know. So, teachers must provide scenarios so they can understand. Each school has a discipline hand book that students are supposed to understand. As a teacher, you should know the student hand book and explain it to the students. Teachers can create an assignment and have students to read the book and answer the questions. The sample I provided is designed to understand school policy. Discipline will be easy to administer because you have taught the students rules. Do not take this for granted. Provide examples from your school handbook. The more students understand the rules the easier it will be to discipline your class. The less they know the rules the more difficult the teacher will be in control. Also, provide extra credit questions about classroom behavior on your next couple of quizzes and/or tests.

How to start and end a class?

It is important to make a grade out of this assignment or student will be reluctant to do it. Do not make it extra credit but an assignment grade. Teachers can make it count 10% of your grade. Whatever works for you? However, I did let them see that it was being graded and they got their grades back.

Chapter 4: Plan & Prepare

Thinking back to your own school days can often help you see the pitfalls of certain teaching techniques. Teachers who were very austere or who were strong disciplinarians did not create a classroom where students wanted to please them but, instead, were scared to fail. Learn by the mistakes of these teachers and try to be the kind of teacher you would have wanted to be taught by.

As middle or high school teachers, we all have good and bad days just like any other human on the planet. It can be hard at times not to bring our issues from outside of the classroom with us into our teaching. Your moods are quickly and easily transferred to others, including your students. If you enter the classroom in a bad mood, then expecting your class to be well behaved and attentive is unrealistic. Instead, make a conscious decision every time you teach, to leave all your baggage at home. The teacher should be happy, full of positive energy and enthusiasm, ready to educate the class in a fun and motivational way.

Equally, as a teacher, you need to remember that your students all have their own problems and emotions that can affect them in class.

Welcoming your Students

From the moment the students step into the classroom, they require you to use management skills. Just forging ahead with the lesson is not a well-planned strategy that will give you good results. The likelihood is that some students will be disinterested, distracted and disruptive and this can quickly spread through the class.

To achieve good classroom management and connect with your students in a way that makes them respect and like you, first, you need to engage with them.

Here is one way that works well with k-12 students. I wish I can apply it with my students at the University of Arizona, but it suits young students more. By greeting each class member by name at the door with a friendly smile and an individual "Hello" "Hi" "How are you doing?" along with a handshake or thumbs up, you are immediately connecting to each and every student verbally, physically and psychologically. By adding an instruction such as "Please sit down quietly" or "Please get into groups of five" and so on, they are helped to transition into a positive learning state of mind. This is especially helpful if students have come from a break such as lunch, as it can take them a while to transition and re-focus on learning. Here is YouTube video of exactly what I am talking about: http://bit.ly/2GqkFuJ

Studies have shown that welcoming students to class can improve student-teacher relationships, increase student engagement and lessen disruptive behavior. It makes each individual feel appreciated and part of the group, which helps them become much more invested in learning.

By starting the class with the individual welcome technique, you immediately create a connection and a feeling of social belonging, which has been proven in research to make students more willing to engage and commit effort towards learning rather than being distracted and disruptive. You will quickly build trust and empathy with your class helping them to feel safe and comfortable in your class.

- When welcoming students remember to:
- Make eye contact.
- Use the student's name in your welcome phrase "Hi Lamia, how's your day going?" or "Hi Aly, how are you today?"
- Use an easy, friendly nonverbal thumbs up, handshake or high five.
- Encourage your students to do something constructive such as getting into groups or sit down quietly.

Making students feel welcome doesn't just benefit the students, it has been shown to lower teacher stress and anxiety and can be beneficial in reducing the incidence of teacher burnout. The reason for this is simple. If students are less disruptive during the class, then the teacher can focus on the real task at hand – teaching their class, rather than having to deal with students' misbehavior. Overall, a healthy, creative, positive working environment should always be created.

Building the Classroom Community

When students are given ways of creating the feeling of community within their classroom, they function far better as a group. They will become invested in not only their own success but the success of their classmates, working together to reach goals and targets presented to them. Don't forget that today's students embrace the 4c's – skills for the 21st century. Collaboration is one of them.

In high school and college, it is very common for students not to know the names of other members of their class, even those they sit next to regularly. To start your classroom community, it is first important that your students know each other. For the first few classes of the year, get your students to write their first names on a sticker and stick these labels onto their pullover or outfit. Arrange the students, not in rows facing forward, but instead in a semicircle or small groups so they can see each other and you. Ask your students to all stand-up and go around the room introducing themselves to each other, stating their name and any likes or interests they have. Allow them enough time so each student can introduce themselves to everyone in the room (this can include you). Then at random ask a few students what they learned about the other students.

This exercise removes the shyness that some students have when interacting with people they don't know. It allows them to feel at ease working and communicating with each other, which is essential when you set group tasks or pairs work. Quickly they learn cooperation, collaboration and how shared investment can be beneficial, contributing to the success of the class as a whole.

Time invested in bringing your class together as a community will be very well spent and be rewarded by dividends very quickly.

You may have heard that it doesn't matter if your students don't like you. You aren't being paid to be their friend, after all, as you are their teacher. However, getting your students to like you will make your job immeasurably easier. You don't have to become their best buddy, but you do have to gain their respect. If your students like you, they will want to please you and will work all the harder to do just that.

What is essential is that your students truly believe you like them. Showing your students respect and giving the same level of attention to all will promote a harmonious working environment.

It is natural to warm to some students more than others, but it is critical that the students are not aware of this and are treated equally.

Ice Breaker

Once you have greeted your students, the next step is to engage with them and capture their attention. You do this by using an "Ice Breaker." Icebreakers help to focus your class and bring their attention toward you rather than toward what their other classmates are doing.

There are several different techniques you can use, and it is best if you mix it up a bit rather than being a "one trick pony." You can:

- Ask students to tell you about something exciting they have been doing. I always begin with this question.
- Share some of your own experiences or funny stories about things that have happened to you or a friend (mentioning no names of course). Students love to hear interesting stories about their teacher. This is particularly beneficial if you

can tie your story into your lesson theme in some way. Prepare it in advance but pretend that it is on the spot.

- Tell a joke but not on a daily basis.
- Perform a magic trick. There are hundreds that are simple to master on YouTube. Check this one: http://bit.ly/2IhYOrc

-

Basically, you just need to engage with your students in some way that they find interesting.

Lesson Topic

Next, tell your students the topic of the lesson today. Try giving it a title that your students can relate to and will find interesting. Write the topic down on the side of the board. Next, instigate a student discussion by asking if they know anything about the topic and write down their responses. You can then expand on these if you like.

Objectives

Next, discuss the objectives or goals of the lesson with the students and write them down under the lesson topic. The more participation you can get from the students, the more engaged they will be with the topic. It also lets them see how well they are doing during the class if you check off the goals as you go along.

Review

Review what was covered in the previous lesson and any correlation it has with the topic of today's lesson. This helps to reinforce prior learning, stimulates the brain, aids recall - which is useful in tests - and creates enthusiasm. Ask students open-ended questions that will help them to remember finer details and test their knowledge and recall.

Class Discussion

Opening the discussion out to the class is a great way to get lots of different views from your students and helps you to measure how well they understand the topic.

Sometimes it can become a little out of control with students all shouting out at once. It's fine to ask your students not to do this but to raise their hands and wait to be asked for their contribution.

When you write the students' answers or opinions, review them with the class and see if they can be expanded upon. Offer feedback and finally add any additional information that was not provided.

Chapter 5: Routines and Procedures

Have you ever been to a school and watched students walk through the hall? Were some classes walking in an orderly and quiet manner? Were other classes walking, running, talking, and being unruly and disturbing other classes? Chances are, the unruly class probably had a teacher with little or no classroom management skills. There were probably no routines or procedures in place either. The teacher with the well-behaved class most likely taught routines and procedures on a daily basis from day one in and out of the classroom. That teacher probably learned about these routines and procedures from books, professional development opportunities, experience in her own classroom, and from watching other seasoned teachers.

Routines and procedures are of extreme importance when working with young students in the elementary setting. Students need structure, rules, routines, and procedures to make it through each and every day of the school year in order to meet their highest learning potential as well as to prevent behavior problems. Routines, procedures, rules, and structure also help keep everyone safe and keep teachers from feeling as though they are going to lose their minds.

Teach the Routine

Classroom management systems are effective because they increase student success by creating an orderly learning environment that improves student academic success and behavior.

By instituting routines and procedures, you create an environment where students know what to expect and how to act. There shouldn't be any surprises in the classroom; the more easily students can slip into the routine each day, they easier your job will be!

When we discussed expectations, we said you need to know what your class should sound like, look like and feel like. The same thought process should go into creating routines and procedures. Envision how your class should enter the room. What will you be doing, what will the students be doing? How will they exit the classroom?

Talk about these processes with your students, let them know what you want to see and hear. It should take conscious effort.

Apply the same process to special procedures. The first time you do something, think about teaching students *how* to complete the task. How to move, where to move, who goes first, how much time they have. How will your students work in groups or partners? How will they get materials for an assignment?

Routines

Students need structure on a daily basis. Teach them the routines of each learning block throughout the day, and eventually, you will not even have to tell them what to do next. For example, students arrive in the morning, unpack, sit at their desk, begin morning work, and wait for announcements. After announcements are over, they complete their morning work, follow procedures for getting a book to read while waiting for others to finish their morning work, and maybe take a reading test on the computer if they are ready. Students will know what to do because they will have practiced it with their teacher over and over. If students sit for too long wondering what to do next or why they haven't moved on to the next part of their day as expected, things most likely will become hectic. They might get antsy, start talking, or exhibiting some type of undesired behavior.

Procedures

How will you handle students when they need a pencil? What about a tissue? What would you do if five students were raising their hands at once for your attention so they could ask you to go to the restroom, get a book to read, to get a sheet of notebook paper, to ask a question, or because they don't feel good? This is a time when procedures save the day!

Another good idea is to have charts in the room stating the procedures for things so students can refer to them if they forget what to do. This will help when a student says, "I didn't know that's what we were supposed to do" or if one says, "I forgot what to do." If you have taught, demonstrated, and practiced the procedures many times *and* have shown them where the charts are to refer to, they have no excuse to not follow procedures. This will cut down on the number of behavior problems that could interrupt instruction during the school day and help more learning take place instead. When you set expectations, it is vitally important to stick to them and to not show partiality to any student. Once you have your expectations set, you can always tweak them to suit your students' personalities and dynamics of the classroom later in the year if necessary.

Chapter 6: Getting to Know Your Students

It is extremely important to get to know your students. Doing this helps you make a necessary and beneficial student/teacher connection. If students are happy in your classroom and they like and respect you because you took the time to get to know them, it sets you up for great relationships and a great school year. Learn about your students on the first day of school! There are many different ways to do this. I have found free printable questionnaires online created specifically for elementary students. Some are more basic than others and only ask for student names, ages, and maybe their favorite food.

Focus on the Positive and Stay Calm

Don't do that! Stop! Quit talking! If you don't behave, I will... This is something most people have heard one or more teachers say to students at some point in their educational experiences. Some people may have also seen a teacher get in students' faces and hover over them with intimidation. There is a more effective and positive method to achieving the desired behavior from students. Over the years, I have witnessed more and more teachers use a positive approach to reaching the desired behavior from their students.

As far as clutter is concerned, get rid of anything that is not a necessity. A clean organized classroom will help make a teacher and the students feel more comfortable and less muddled. For example, if there is a learning center on a shelf along with other things like wet wipes, empty baskets, or broken pencils mixed with the learning center materials, students might wonder what the other items are doing there and begin to question you while you are trying to work with other students at your teacher-led center. This causes disruptions and interrupts the learning process. Therefore, it is best to keep only the learning materials in a center, and everything else in a tidy storage area or in the garbage.

Good seating and room arrangements help with behavior issues, students who have trouble seeing the board, and when there is a need to have a student sit near the teacher for various reasons. Also, transitioning from each learning center or just walking around the room in general should be an easy process. It should not be difficult to walk throughout the classroom. For example, some areas of the room might have items in the way that could cause someone to trip, or one might have to squeeze through a tight area to get to their destination. Plenty of room should be between student chairs as well if they are sitting back-to-back to prevent them from bumping each other when standing up and pushing in their chairs. A well-arranged room will help everyone transition through different times of the school day and will help prevent trips and falls.

Planning for Effective Learning and Structure

Have you ever walked into a classroom and been shocked at the chaos going on? It's noisy, the teacher is scrambling to get ready for a lesson, and students are walking around trying to find a book or something to do because they are finished with their work and are waiting on the teacher. I have witnessed this several times. This is due to poor planning and no structure. To prevent times like this, create a daily schedule and stick to it! Also, have your lessons prepared and ready to go ahead of time. Have all the materials you need for the lesson, so you are not left searching for them or preparing them while the students are in the classroom waiting for you to teach. Being prepared ahead of time will ensure maximum instructional time, more effective learning, and better classroom management.

Why kids misbehave?

The number one reason most students misbehave in a classroom is because the teacher does not have anything for the student to do. In other words, the teacher is not prepared. The teacher is not organized. The teacher is not a good manager or ruler. When I say prepared, the effective teacher must have the entire day planned from beginning to end. The effective teacher must have everyday planned even up until the last day of school. The effective teacher must be in control of every second or treason is bound to happen. Let not one minute of your day go unaccounted for without having something for your students to do. Yes, at first this will seem like a lot of work, but it is much easier than teacher think. I did not say that teachers had to teach every second, but teachers must be in control every second.

First, do not be the teacher that comes to class late. You are building a reputation. Do not send a student to the office to make copies for you. Do not ask the secretary or someone in the office to run off copies so the students will have something to do because you are not prepared. Always have stay head. This is a red flag. The student returns to make copies and copy machine is broken and then the teachers begin to panic because there is nothing for the students to do. It will happen, so stay ahead of the game and do everything in advance.

The second reason why a classroom misbehaves is because the teacher talks too much. Kings do not talk they rule. They point their finger. I hear teachers all the time talking about how their throat hurts and how their knees hurt. Stop talking all the time and sit down on your throne and direct your servants to do the work for you. Talk less and rule more. Have students to read the directions. Do not move all those desks; have a student move the desk. Rule, Rule, Rule, Rule! Do not erase the board, have a student to erase the board. Every time a teacher does something think to yourself can I get a student to do it? More importantly, can I get a student to do it orderly? Train your servants to do things. Explain it to them over and over and then let them do it. Then, have a student to correct them when they do it wrong. Have you ever seen a king in the field doing work? Do not read a book every period for six periods a day. Record the book on a tape once and play it aloud each period. Order the book on tape; ask the assistant principal early to pay for the audio book for you. Video tape teaching difficult assignments and play it again the next day. The media center has all the equipment and the students will be more than happy to record it. Show short video clips of everything you teach. There are programs out their called United Streaming that shows short video clips on no matter what subject you are teaching. Why teach all the math problems when teachers can go on YouTube and watch the clip. Keep your army busy; no free time ever. If teachers watch a movie, the students must take notes. Teachers do not have to grade all of them. Add questions from the movie on your next assignment. Your energy level is not like theirs. They have 10 times more energy than you. Plus, they want to do stuff. Let them do it. Remember, kids often misbehave because they do not have anything to do. Let them do it.

Chapter 7: Discipline & Regulate

We have touched on some reasons why students might be disruptive in class. Everyone is different, and all have their own struggles to deal with on a day to day basis. It is very likely you won't be aware of your student's lives outside of school and the difficulties they may face. Simply assuming a student is bad because they are not well behaved in class could mean they are struggling elsewhere and not just in school. Adolescents dealing with changing hormone levels and developing bodies often have problems controlling and understanding their emotions.

Causes of Disruptive Behavior

When one student starts misbehaving in a classroom, very rapidly it can spread to affect other students too. Trying to stop this with punishment can backfire as students then harbor resentment of the punishment and are more likely to misbehave further rather than comply.

The best way to prevent bad behavior in class is by preventing it from happening to start with. There are several ways to achieve this:

- Create a classroom environment that engages students and keeps them focused and interested.
- Be approachable, friendly and communicative with your students. Allow them to connect and build a rapport with you and feel comfortable asking for your help.
- Don't allow attention gaps where students do not have something to occupy themselves. If they complete a task, ensure they are provided with something else to do, such as revising a previous lesson or starting on their homework.
- Allocate student roles to give them some responsibility in the class.
- Focus and reward positive conduct rather than punishing bad behavior.
- Allow students to establish their own classroom guidelines. They are far more likely to stick to "the rules" if they made them themselves.
- Ask students to sign a contract agreeing that they will abide by the guidelines put forward to them by the teacher.
- Document the classroom guidelines and revisit them as part of your class warmup in the lesson introduction.
- Ensure the guidelines are listed in order of importance.

- Allow the students to choose appropriate consequences for misconduct.
- Display the class guidelines in a prominent place where all the class can see them clearly.
- Allow the students to make suggestions for changes, additions and amendments to the classroom guidelines.
- Don't make the guideline list too long or too complex. Keep the list short and focus on what is most important.
- Never punish the entire class for one student's misconduct.

If an argument breaks out in class between students, ask the students to do a role play between themselves to demonstrate how they could have handled the situation in a more acceptable manner.

Important Guidelines

There are several important guidelines that need to be included in the class rules. If the students don't mention these when creating their list, then bring them up as suggestions explaining why they are important.

- Mobile phones and other electrical devices must be turned off and put away in bags before entering the classroom. They must remain there until students exit the class unless they are expressly asked to use them as part of an exercise.
- Treat all other class members respectfully.
- Be responsible for the care of classroom property.
- Don't shout out in class but raise your hand if you would like to speak.
- Ask for help if you don't understand.
- If the class is engaged in group activities, it can become quite noisy. Rather than trying to make yourself heard above this, try using a nonverbal signal such as flashing the classroom lights on and off to get the students' attention.
- If a student frequently causes disruption in class, take that student aside and discuss it with them in a friendly and understanding manner. Explain why their behavior is disruptive to the rest of the class and ask them how they can address the problem. By getting the student involved in a positive way, you are far more likely to solve the issue and prevent further occurrence.
- Be sure to spread your praise equally among your students and not always pick the same ones. Resentment can build up if you don't share your rewards fairly.

- If, despite all your effort, a student continues to be unruly, then contact their parents and ask them in for a meeting with the student present to discuss the situation or use the student counselor to help mediate the problem.

- Never be confrontational. If a student is talking in class, it is better to ask them "Do you have a question?" rather than say "Stop talking, you're disrupting the class." Or "Do you need some help with the assignment?" rather than "Stop messing around."

- Chastising students in front of their classmates can build resentments. Instead, take them aside and talk with them privately.

- Have some empathy with your students. At the end of the day, we are all human and make mistakes, have good and bad days and outside issues that can affect our performance. This is true not only for the student but also for you as a teacher.

Coping with Children with Particular Needs

Children who are persistently defiant or difficult in a class may have more to deal with than others. They could have an attention disorder or a learning disorder or an anger disorder.

These can manifest themselves in ways that frequently disturb your class including:

- Hostility towards the teacher or other students.
- Persistent defiance.
- Explosions of anger.
- Continually annoying other students.
- Arguing.
- Blaming others.
- Emotional episodes.

How can you best deal with students with these problems?

Keep Calm

If a student is angry then the fastest way of dissipating the anger is to be very, very calm. Even if the student has been rude and has upset you, do not rise to their anger level. Maintain a calm gentle positive tone of voice, keep your body language neutral with your hands by your sides and don't enter the student's personal space.

Chapter 8: Demonstrate & Guide

All students require guidance and, as an educator, it is necessary to ensure that all members of a class gain as much help as they need. If a student is finding a subject difficult, they are far more likely to become bored, disinterested and disruptive to the rest of the class.

Learning by Example

By modeling good behavior through acting and talking to your students in the same way that you want your students to behave, you will subconsciously influence them. This can be done by:

- Smiling and using a friendly approach.
- Showing gratitude.
- Maintaining eye contact.
- Using polite and appropriate language.
- Not interrupting people when they are speaking.
- Setting basic rules about how to treat each other in class.

Demonstrating how things are done to students does not stop there. Part of introducing any new idea in a lesson involves the teacher modeling it. This requires you to give a demonstration of what is required. You have several choices here. You can choose to model before the students attempt to complete a task or you can let them do it first, and model after they have finished, which will mean they are more likely to make mistakes.

The merit of modeling before allowing students to attempt a task is that they will feel more confident about it, understand what is required and are more likely to return the expected results. However, sometimes it can also be good to allow the students to complete the task before you model it because it makes them think a lot harder. They may be unsure of what exactly you are expecting and will often be more creative and think outside of the box. After all, there will be few occasions in life when they will have any tasks they are given modeled to them. They will often be required to solve problems on their own. This method is often far more engaging for the students, and although they may not always get things right the first time, they will find the challenge far more interesting.

If you use the strategy of modeling after the event, then you can also opt not to do the modeling yourself. It may be that a student or group of students performed the task well, and you can ask them to demonstrate their findings to the class.

Giving Assistance

In modern teaching, students are encouraged to explore information in a variety of different ways and to connect to learning using many different techniques. Teachers should not try to dominate their class, but as facilitators to different ways of learning, they should be observers who assist their students when it is required. This essentially means allowing students to discover self-directed learning. The best way to do this is to really get to know your students as well as you can. In primary school this is simple, but it is a lot harder when you only see students once or twice a week in high-school or college. This, however, can be overcome through individual study, group and pair work because it helps students to self-support and be exposed to different learning strategies.

Practice Makes Perfect

Reviewing material that has already been covered is an essential practice. For a student to truly absorb and be able to recall information quickly and accurately, it needs to be moved into their long-term memory. The most effective way of doing this is to revisit the information in different ways frequently. This is to some extent done at the beginning of the class when the teacher asks the students about what they did in the previous lesson, but there are ways of including elements of prior learning during the lesson, and these should be included as often as possible. It takes a minimum of three times for a student to fully absorb information given.

Check for Understanding

If you don't know if your students understand the topic they are learning, how can you be sure they get it? Checking for understanding can be done in many ways including formative and summative assessment. The use of long-term projects, class quizzes, open discussions, presentation, and homework are all ways of measuring your students' understanding and pinpointing those students who require more help.

Feedback

Once you know where your students' individual strengths and weaknesses are, you can start to give feedback to help them. Rather than just giving a student feedback on how they might improve their current topic of work, try to focus more on giving feedback that will help the student, in general, to do a better job overall. That way, the student will be able to improve their marks overall and not just in one small area.

Self-Evaluation

This is another way to help students to self-educate. By allowing students to evaluate their own work and explain how they would then improve upon it - having seen how other students approached the same problem - will help to make them more autonomous.

Creating Behavioral Routine

Although using different and varied ways of learning is very important to keep students interested, what is also important is some level of routine. We are creatures of habit and, once formed, habits are hard to break, so the best method is to create good habits right from the beginning. Always keep the routine at the beginning of your class the same. Welcome students, give them a direction (sit quietly, get out a certain book, etc.), tell them about the topic of the day and the objectives and discuss what was learned in the previous lesson. This kind of familiar routine allows students to become settled before the real teaching of the lesson begins. Ending the class in the same way each time is also beneficial. You should ask if any student has anything they would like to ask about the lesson today and set their homework, ensuring they write down what the homework is.

Guided Practice

When teaching an entirely new topic, such as introducing a math class to algebra, for example, it will be necessary to give students a lot of attention before requiring them to prove their understanding. Many examples should be given, and you should ask class members to answer questions along the way to show whether they understand. Moving onto independent practice too quickly will cause students to make a lot more mistakes and will discourage any who have not grasped the key concepts. Be careful not to try to make your students run before they can walk. Use lots of modeling, guided practice, group practice, and pair work first. Also be sure to regularly check to see if your students understand.

Supporting your students is of vital importance if they are to succeed. It is important to frequently re-iterate to students that it is perfectly okay for them to ask for help, or to question you further or request more information. Let them understand that this is encouraged and is not a negative approach.

Chapter 21: Motivate & Reward

Once you have gained your class's attention, you can start to motivate them toward learning the topic of the day.

Many teachers find motivating their students difficult, but it is a very important aspect of being a teacher because unmotivated students don't learn effectively. To make your classes interesting, make them interactive. Simply build this into your lesson plans for a stress-free class. We will look at ways of doing this below.

For a student to retain information and become an eager and willing participant in the classroom, you will need a skill set that includes knowing how to:

- Praise and encourage your students.
- Involve the class in the topic you are teaching.
- Give incentives.
- Be creative.
- Keep it real.

By using these techniques, you will help to keep your students self-motivated, so they are enjoying their learning. It will help to ensure they reach their full potential.

Praise and Encourage

Let your students know when they are doing things well, and even when they aren't. Rather than chastise them, try instead to help them and use encouraging language to stimulate their desire to do more. Allow a flow of open communication so your students feel they can talk with you and express any difficulties. Students can feel embarrassed if they don't understand something, so make sure they know it's perfectly alright to ask for help. By making your classroom into a place with a friendly atmosphere where your students respect you and each other and that, in return, you respect them; they will be more comfortable and open to learning. Praise individuals in the class often. A "Good job!" compliment can go a long way and encourage even better work in the future.

Encourage Involvement

By giving students specific jobs such as being responsible for handing out worksheets or cleaning the board at the end of the lesson and so on, you make them part of what's happening. For any reading out loud, ensure you allow the class members to take turns and keep the sections each student reads short. Remember that some children don't like reading out loud, so offer plenty of encouragement and be sure to let them know they did well when they finish.

When assigning group work, give each member of the group a role. This will give them a sense of responsibility and accomplishment and encourages them to participate actively in the class.

Use Incentives

Rewarding students who do well can make them more productive because it motivates them and gives them a feeling of achievement. Receiving rewards makes students happy.

However, using "bribes" is a big no-go area. Bribing students by saying "If you do X well, I will give you Y" isn't a good way to work. It is not a positive reinforcement but a negative one. This is because their attention isn't on the task in hand. They have no interest in the task itself as their focus is on the reward.

A better strategy is to surprise students with occasional rewards for a job well done. For instance, giving a student a certificate of achievement if that student has shown continued and consistent improvement in their work, or attained a particularly good score for an assignment that they clearly put a lot of time and effort into. By rewarding after the fact, students don't focus on the reward, as they don't know they are getting one.

Remember also that words of praise especially in front of the class, are a great motivator. Be mindful to notice and reward the improvements made by weaker students as well as those who find lessons easy.

Writing a personal letter to the parents of children who have made a marked improvement is also a good incentive.

Be Creative

Rather than always keeping the structure of your class the same, change things up a bit and keep your classes fresh and interesting. Students enjoy playing learning games rather than copying endless notes from the board or listening to long lectures. Use lots of visual aids, class participation, debating, colorful handouts, video recordings and so on. A sterile classroom environment can be psychologically negative to learning. If you have your own classroom, then decorate it with the students' work. This lets students see you appreciate and celebrate their work and it strengthens their feeling of belonging.

Keep it real

Many older students think much of what they are forced to learn is pointless and will question when they will ever need to know about it in "real life." To negate this, use realistic situations to demonstrate why what you are teaching is relevant and important. Use examples of real people in real jobs utilizing the information you are teaching. Also, show how it could be useful to know just for their own benefit at home. You can get the students to play act realistic situations, where appropriate, which they find great fun.

Assessments

When doing informal and formative assessments, rather than giving a classic A to F score, just tell the students if they did or did not meet with your expectations. Receiving a paper marked with a big red F will not inspire a struggling student to try harder. It will demotivate them and likely stop them from trying altogether. Those who did not meet with your expectations must then be given help. This can be done by reviewing the key material in a different way, doing pair work where you team up a weaker student with a stronger one or group work, so students support each other. When you do a new assessment, make sure that they now understand. If they don't, spend some one on one time with them while other students are doing independent or group study in class. Often it only takes a few minutes for you to clarify the problem. You can also deploy the compliment technique as follows: "I'm really pleased with your work on X. You're doing great. Would you like some help with Y?"

Try utilizing these techniques in your classroom and mix things up a bit. Be a creative and inspirational teacher and not only will your students have a fun time learning, but you'll have a fun time teaching.

Have students to practice lining up

As simple as this may sound, doing this with the wrong group of students will be chaotic. If you just tell a group of early middle school kids to line up. There will a mad race to see who is going to be the first in line. Students will begin to skip each other in the line and pulling on each other shoving telling students to get behind them. This can cause fights and believe me a lot of fussing. Do not leave anything out for granted.

This is why teachers practice with your student to go places. Practice for a fire drill before the actual fire drill. Practice how to go to the library and what the teacher expects the student to do before they go to the library. Show students around the library and explain the procedures. Take students to the physical education and explain the procedures. Where will students go if it is raining and there is no ramp or hall way. Take time during the first two weeks of school and practice.

Emergency lesson plans and classroom assignments

Most teachers are required to provide lesson plans when they are out of class. An ineffective teacher will want the substitute to be a teacher and continue with the same lesson.

The teacher is out for three days, can you imagine all the work the teacher will have to grade and record? Imagine the students who talked the substitute into going to the gym? How are you going to account for them? I only give extra credit to students who were did the assignments as required. I look to see how many problems the student did and I base it on that. I also take point off for students who did not complete the assignment. I do not want them to think that it is a day off from work when the teacher is not there. Besides, the king is off not the servants. I do not grade work when I am out; I just give credit for doing it.

Chapter 10: Stimulate & Inspire

There are various ways to stimulate and inspire students. By doing so, you will further encourage each member of your class to want to achieve more. This desire to achieve further strengthens the classroom community and everyone's respect for each other.

The Social Class

When students work in pairs or groups, they learn from one another. This peer-to-peer collaboration is a great way to discover new ideas and think of things in different ways. To promote this way of learning, rather than using traditional classroom seating plans when all the chairs face front, try grouping students around tables in small groups facing each other or use a horseshoe configuration so everyone is facing each other but can still clearly see the board. This generates a feeling of togetherness and unity. Also try allowing students to move around in the classroom, by giving them exercises that require them to walk about and communicate with each other. This way of learning is fun and effective.

Encourage and Support Initiative

In mixed ability classes, there are often some children who achieve tasks more quickly and easily than others. Rather than allowing them to sit and become restless, it is better to allow them to either help other students who may be struggling to complete the task or to work ahead if appropriate.

Nonverbal Teaching

We think of nonverbal communication in daily life to mean gestures such as smiling, giving a thumbs up or touching someone's arm in a gesture of support or agreement. But in an educational environment nonverbal communication can mean a whole lot more.

Nonverbal teaching stimulates your students' brains differently. This is good because it allows you the opportunity to offer students who learn in a kinesthetic, auditory, or visual way equal opportunity to learn. A class who are sitting listening to the teacher talk about a subject that is not engaging are likely to zone out and absorb little if any of what they are being told. Even if they then go on two write notes about it, chances are they will still only retain a small fraction of the information. By teaching the same information using nonverbal techniques suddenly the learning is stimulating and easy to absorb and remember for the vast majority of students. Examples of nonverbal teaching include:

Learning Stations – Where students move in groups through a series of learning stations around the classroom. Each station has a different activity based on the subject being taught. Examples of this could be a station where students watch a short video, one where they must solve a series of problems by combining their collective knowledge, one where they must complete a creative activity and one where they must create a small presentation about the subject to perform. The use of props, worksheets, video, performance, and creation all stimulate and inspire students. The more varied the activities are at each station, the better. This is because it allows the information to be learned in many different ways, making it fun and more interesting for the students.

Task Cards – This is another activity that can be done in small groups. Give each group a set of cards that each have different problems for them to solve. The cards should include words and pictures if possible. When the group has completed the tasks on all the cards, they can then move on to the next set of cards until all the groups have answered all the cards. You can add interest by making it into a competition where the group who get the most cards correct can win a prize at the end.

Think Pair Share –Students are then paired up, so they can discuss their thoughts and ideas. Each pair then presents their findings to the class. Finally, the class is asked for their thoughts.

Grouping Students – As we have already seen, students learn in different ways. Each individual will have their own way of learning, be it visual, auditory or kinesthetic. It is useful to note that most students are kinesthetic learners, meaning they best absorb new information through activities and not from writing notes from the board. When you get to know your students, you will be able to recognize those who learn in a particular way. By grouping these together, you allow like-minded students to share their learning experience, giving you the opportunity to move around and spend time with each group.

Open-Ended Projects – Rather than setting just one fixed project or style of project, try offering your students several options for their open-ended projects. This allows them to choose one that they feel best demonstrates their knowledge. Ensure you include a clear rubric so that expectations are clearly defined.

Student Lead Activity

Students often enjoy taking on the role of the teacher and giving a short presentation on what they have learned. This allows them to practice their recall and gives you the chance to do a quick formative assessment, so you know if the student has clearly understood the subject.

Sharing Strengths and Weaknesses

By sharing your own strengths and weaknesses with the class, students can learn that not everyone learns and processes information in the same way. It lets them see that you, as a teacher, are not infallible and that you also have difficulty with certain things. This will help inspire your students as they see you as a role model and they will find it encouraging that you are not perfect, but simply human.

As you can see, there are many ways to stimulate and inspire your class. I'm sure you will be able to think up many more.

Chapter 11: How to Establish Classroom Rules and Expectations

 The popular advice usually given with regards to classroom rules and expectations is to have clear expectations/rules and to post them somewhere on the wall in your classroom. Keep your expectations simple and only have three to five. Students won't remember any more than that and if you have a big long list of rules they will just tune you out anyways. Some teachers get caught in the trap of thinking they must have a rule for every possible situation that may come up in a classroom. No you don't! Have three main ones and then explain to the class that the rest are common sense. Here is a list of rules that in my opinion everybody already knows.

-Don't talk while the teacher is talking

-raise your hand if you have a question

-ask to go to the bathroom

-don't answer your cellphone in class

-no swearing

-cheating isn't allowed

-be on time to class

 There are so many more, but I think you get the picture. I personally think it is insulting to the kid to put a big long list of rules up on the wall. The kids who are going to break the rules are going to do so whether you have a list on your wall or not, same with the kids that are going to follow the rules.

Establish your three main rules on the first day. Let the kids know that we all know the rules of a classroom since we have all been going to school for years and those same rules apply in your classroom. You can even give a few examples if you like but most kids aren't stupid, and they know. If you have one or two rules that are out of the ordinary than maybe you want to key on those. How you enforce the rules is the real key not how you make them or if you have them posted on your wall.

Get a Routine

Routine is good. Most kids thrive under routine. Heck most people in general do! So set up a routine in your classroom. If you teach in elementary than you will have a daily routine and if you teach middle school or high school than you will have a class routine for each class, you teach. Routine doesn't necessarily just have to pertain to what or when you do things each class it also pertains to how you run your class and how you administer discipline and uphold your expectations. Students like to know what to expect especially when it comes to classroom management. A routine will make it easier for you to enforce your expectations and it will help your students to follow your expectations and future students also. As a teacher, you gain a reputation in a school. Whether your routine is positive or negative you will fall into a routine. If your routine is reactive and you don't consistently reinforce your expectations word will get out and you will have a reputation that precedes you when you have a new class with new kids. This can put you behind the eight-ball before you even start in terms of classroom management. If you have a routine of being proactive with regards to your classroom management and expectations are consistently upheld, then future students will know, and it will be that much easier to establish yourself with your new class because they already have an expectation of you and your competence in the classroom.

As to how much routine you put into your classroom that is up to the individual. Some people need to have more of a routine then others. I heard a guy give a talk on classroom management and he said we should meet our students at the door and shake each of their hands as they came in. No thanks! I do not have the time, nor do I want to touch their hands with   hands. For one I don't know where their hands have been and some of them just look gross, haven't showered and just having them in class is enough. My point is figure out what is right for you.

Being Proactive Rather Than Reactive

You see that phrase and you think that makes sense. Nobody in their right mind would argue with it. However, you'd be surprised how many people don't live by it. It's the whole idea of the path of least resistance. Sometimes you are tired, or you are tired of dealing with the behavior and it is easier to ignore it than to deal with it. What is the harm anyways? At the beginning of the year or semester before you have firmly established your classroom management routine, I would say there is lots of harm in letting things slide. Things are allowed to slide until you can't deal with it anymore and then you react! When you are being reactive is when bad things can happen because emotions are involved. This is when you say or do something you wish you could take back!

How to Gain the Respect of Your Class

If your students don't respect you than chances are high that you are going to be in for a rough year. Some teachers get the idea of being respected and being liked confused. You don't need your students to like you, but you do need them to respect you. Usually the two go hand in hand and in my opinion classroom management is easier when you as the teacher are both respected and liked. However, if you can only achieve one of them then it is better to be respected.

There is also the idea of making an example of someone in the class. I don't mean that you just simply pick on a kid for the sake of making an example to the rest of the class.

Good Planning Often Results in Good Classroom Management

This is pretty self-explanatory. There is a saying these days when talking about internet marketing and websites that content is king. This is the same in teaching. I am not going to go into how to put together a lesson plan. However, the more engaging your content is or in other words, what you do in the classroom, the less classroom management issues you will have to deal with. Like I said before, strong classroom management can even compensate for a poor lesson plan but any teacher worth their salt will be constantly trying to deliver better and more compelling content.

Chapter 12: Creating a Structured Classroom

A structured classroom is the key to building an environment in which all participants feel comfortable, productive and calm. In this book I will describe the five elements that will help you build a plan that addresses the needs of your students, your school, your student's parents and yourself.

Remember, to take care of others, you first need to take care of yourself; so, as we move through these ideas, think about what works for you. Think about your students, your space, and most of all your sanity.

Although classroom management can be time consuming and labor intensive to start, the most successful teachers invest the time, planning and effort in the beginning, which pays huge dividends throughout the school year.

Classroom management does not happen overnight. It's a system that you develop and adapt to meet the needs of your classroom, your students and their needs.

In fact, what works for one class period, may not work for the others. It is vital that you take into account the needs of individual learners when building your plan. You may have the perfect plan on paper but when your students walk in the classroom you could decide to try something else completely. That's perfectly acceptable. These things take trial, error and practice.

Start with the Rules

Who makes the rules? Well, you do. Your classroom is your community, and that community should be a democracy. You are the leader, but it takes input from all stakeholders to create an environment where everyone feels welcomed, valued and accepted. No easy feat.

So, to start, you have to define your expectations. What do you want to see, hear, and feel each day in your classroom? For example, we expect to *see* students arriving on time. We would like to *hear* students speaking respectfully to each other. We should all *feel* like we are part of a team.

Your rules are best written in a positive statement. "Be polite." "Respect each other." This is where you can involve your students in the decision-making. Students who have contributed to the list of rules will have more ownership of them and their effects.

Different classes may have different needs. Maybe you have your non-negotiables, and each class gets to add two. This is how you build community; involving the constituents in the conversation.

Next, you need to communicate these rules to your people; parents and students. The rules should be direct, and they should be constantly reviewed and inserted into daily classroom conversations.

Post your rules in the room so you can refer to them easily when they are, or are not, being followed. Students need constant reminders of your expectations.

For example, a student pokes another student. Point to the rule the student violated. Ask them to read it, ask how they violated the rule and together you should discuss how this behavior should be avoided in the future.

The rules should also be communicated to your student's parents. It's important for parents to know your expectations so that they can support their students and support you if they are broken.

Be consistent and make sure you follow through. This is what makes your classroom effective. Students know that you will enforce the rules, for every student, all the time. You are the teacher who treats everyone the same. Successful teachers stick to the rules, and so do their students.

Remember, keep it short, be direct and maintain consistency.

Consequences

So, once you have set up your ideal systems, what happens when they just don't listen? This is when you have to start enforcing consequences.

First, let's talk about positive reinforcements. It's important to highlight when kids are doing the *right* thing. Tell them when they are doing well. This doesn't come naturally to everyone.

Students crave praise; especially the unsuspecting ones. How will your most difficult student react when you start to praise him/her instead of admonishing them? Start to look for the actions your students are doing well; you might be surprised what you see.

Negative interactions, although easier to recognize are more difficult to manage. Always remember to keep your cool. You are the adult; never forget that. And, that *does* mean that you are in charge, it *does not* mean you should abuse your power.

When students act out, be sure not to glamorize anything against the rules. Make it a point to talk to students in a calm voice, and not always in front of the whole class. As hard as it will be, maintain your composure in front of the group. If you need to count to ten or ask the student to meet you at the door, do that. But don't give them the reaction they are craving.

If a student continues to disobey, follow up with the consequences. Be clear in your expectations, how to change the behavior and what happens next. Changing behavior is the key; remind them they can make better decisions and how. This is also where you will need to communicate with parents on the next steps and the punishment.

Chapter 13: Relationship Matter

Students are looking for teachers who care. You can show you care by being consistent, following through with what you say, and developing a plan for students to be successful. The most caring teachers want their students to succeed; but you have to be willing to give the students the tools they need so that you can work together in harmony.

To build relationships with students, students must know that you respect them as learners, and you care about their interests. What are some strategies you can use to get to know your students? Think about some information exchanges to start the school year.

Many teachers use a questionnaire or a modified version of BINGO so that they can learn their students, and students can learn about each other. Teachers who want to build a community also engage students in team building activities or interview sessions with each other. This is not a waste of instructional time. This is relationship building, which allows students to be authentic. It also allows them to see you as a human; not just a teacher.

As your students grow and mature throughout the year, revisit their likes and dislikes again. Your students are going to change and grow so much in one year. What they like in August will surely not be the same by February.

Also, take interest in their activities outside of the school day; attend sporting events and performances. Students perform for teachers who care.

What are some ways you can show students you care, while maintaining high expectations? Again, relationships are not about being liked. They are about mutual respect; and nothing shows respect like going out of your way to make sure you know about their interests.

Engagement

The most successful teachers do not allow their students down time. Each minute is focused on the learning targets for that day. These teachers have a structured agenda, which they follow, and students learn to expect. The best classes are the ones where students are not hanging on, waiting for the bell to ring!

Participation should not be an option. A student who never knows when it will be their turn to share, has to stay engaged in the conversation in order to keep up. This is why it's important to make participation a non-negotiable. If you use an electronic or random system that helps you choose participants in a fair way, students will also anticipate the game like situation.

Use small groups to get students to interact with each other. They can come to consensus on an answer and share out. This allows you to not only engage students in discussion and collaboration, but it gives you a chance to check for understanding as you listen to them talk and share out their answers. Small whiteboards are also helpful for these activities.

In middle school, autonomy is an integral component of development. Choice and interest can be determining factors for the learning environment. Students who have the feeling that they are choosing what to do, feel more confident in the task they are completing, whether they get it all right or not. Giving the constituents a say gives them ownership in the community.

Incorporating movement can also help those rambunctious little bodies stay focused. Once you have taught them how, let them move around the room. Teach them "Four Corners "with multiple choice answers. Use "Agree or Disagree "statements and make students choose a side of the room. Rotate the student's seats so that they interact with new people. This gives students a chance to engage another part of their brain, and movement wakes up sleepy neurons.

Engagement also means offering varying levels of difficulty so that students have opportunities for success. Some activities that involve movement and the whole class may not have the rigor of partner work, which involves inquiry or experimentation. Not everything has to be at the most difficult task. Sometimes a simple task can get kids to think just as hard.

Chapter 14: Entering the Classroom

This is the time when kids can be at their most disruptive. Try to totally ignore what is going on in the class and calmly take you place in front of them, preparing whatever it is that you have to prepare. The children are expecting to be shouted at, but this isn't always going to be the best way forward. Male teachers who have a loud voice and a lot of authority tend to shout and they may be listened to, but believe me, it's a better way forward to simply sit at your desk and look toward the class, waiting for the children to make the right move. If this takes a long time, some kids will ask why you are not teaching them, and your answer can be very clear. "When you are all settled, I will begin." This prompts kids to police kids, which means that among themselves, they decide that it's more productive to actually knuckle down than to sit there and learn nothing. You can even take a book into class with you if you believe this will give you a distraction. Kids will want to know what your intentions are, but while they are rowdy, there's not much point in trying to get their attention. If you try and fail, you end up being another teacher who let them down.

When you have the attention of the children, decide where you would like kids to be seated. By this time, you will have an idea of who is disruptive and who is not and can seat the disruptive children at the front of the class where you can keep a close eye on them. Kids don't like being singled out and being made to look foolish but apart from moving the kids to different places, you can also use this exercise to group your children so that each group has a natural leader. This is helpful for projects where kids are encouraged to work together. I remember one teacher doing this and choosing a weaker child as a team leader and the other kids questioned it. "I have my reasons," she explained and by the end of the class, the kids were glad she had chosen as she had. This kid was particularly good at explaining things to other students and the team run by him were the first to hand in their results. It also helps for kids to be able to see that different character traits don't make another kid weak or strong. They simply mean that the child approaches life from a different stance. With bullying being rife in schools, it's very important that teachers do not contribute to bullying and that they encourage kids to mix together and to gain benefits from doing so.

If you know that you have a disruptive class in advance, you can re-arrange the seating so that when the kids arrive, you are already there and can direct them to their intended seats. They won't be expecting this and sometimes it works really well in favor of learning because you are able to distance disruptive kids from each other. Kids that want to learn but who are unable to because of the noise of other kids should also be given seats where they are more likely to be able to ask questions as the class progresses.

Knowing the Kids in Your Class

One of the major complaints that kids come up with about teachers is that they don't care about them. Kids are only their problem within the schoolroom, and they don't care that the kids have to go home to bad circumstances or lives that are far from ideal. I would suggest that on the first day you teach a class that is known to be disruptive that you take a little time aside and talk to your students. Let them know who you are and what interests you and then get each child in turn to announce his/her name and tell the class a little about their background or family or even their interests. This serves several purposes. During the course of the introduction you get to see which kids the leaders of the pack are and who are the timid students. You also get to understand their attitudes a little better and this will help you in your classwork to determine which method of teaching to use. There are going to be a mixed bag of kids. Some will grasp ideas quickly and be quite bigheaded about their achievements while others will be slow. If you introduce kids to each other and always group them so that those who are able to mentor them cater for slow kids, you create an atmosphere of empathy and that's really important. Each child has his/her place in the pecking order, and it's your job, as a teacher, to make each child recognize his/her strengths and weaknesses and use them as a group so that you get the most effective teaching methods in place to cater for all.

You are also going to get to know which kids are happy to run around for the teacher, giving out books, *etc.* but these are not always the obvious choices. If you have kids who are disruptive, they can be used as well to occupy their minds and to show them that even though they are trying to disrupt the class, they are expected to conform to the activities that go on in the class.

You may be very nervous when you enter a class for the first time. Kids can do that to you, but you have to keep your chin up and you need to show the class that you don't respond to intimidation and that you are in fact, oblivious to it. By being neutral at all times, and not picking on the obvious kids that deserve it, you are teaching children that this kind of behavior is intolerable and that you are there for every child in the class, regardless of their temperament.

Getting the Attention of the Class

A lot of teachers make the mistake of giving out too many instructions too quickly. "Please sit down, stop talking and open your text book at page 29" is too much instruction in one go. Kids may sit down. They may become quieter, but they will have already forgotten which page you asked them to open. You need to have the children seated and have their attention before you start the lesson. "I want all eyes on me!" is a good way to do it because the kids tend to wonder what's coming next and they are probably looking in your direction anyway so it's not a great deal of effort for them. Then, if a child is still standing, use your head to signal to him to sit down. Don't resort to shouting. Shouting doesn't show you as being strong. It shows you to be intolerant and incapable of dealing with things in a calm way. Once you show kids that you can be riled, believe me, they will do all they can to rile you.

Teaching isn't about you being in charge. It's about you being able to impart information to your students that allows them to pass their examinations. If you find that the kids are bored with the idea of the curriculum from the first day, you are going to experience resistance. There's a better way to deal with this.

Finding out the kid's interests

Talk to the kids about why they don't particularly like the subject that you have to teach them. Encourage discourse between you so that you get a better idea of what methods would work with the students. For example, if you are teaching history, they may not enjoy the subject because they may not see the relevance to their lives. You may be able to introduce costumes or take them on an excursion that opens up their ideas about the subject. There may be ways that you can gain their interest. Think of what their lives are all about and try to make some relationship between their interests and the subjects that you are teaching. For example, a math teacher would be able to explain that in order to buy the latest iPod at a good price, you need to understand all about bartering and value for money and that's where math comes in.

An English teacher who is trying to explain the meaning of poetry to a class may come up with resistance because the kids don't see the relevance. Make it relevant. One teacher in our school got the kids to write out poems for themselves trying to make the meaning clear of classic poems so that it became relevant to the kids and they remembered what those classic poems meant. It was actually quite amusing to hear Shakespeare in rap, but it served a very good purpose because the lessons were easier for the kids to understand without having to be boring.

You get the attention of your class by LISTENING. You also get the attention of the class by understanding you are only a very small part of that child's day. You can make a difference to the child's life or to the child's future by seeing things in perspective and by realizing that a superior stance won't help. In fact, it may alienate kids because they see your world and their world as two different places. When you find a middle ground, you will be able to teach the kids in a better way that suits them and that opens up your ability to teach different sectors of the community. That's valuable experience.

Friendships

Be very aware that you are not a friend or family member to these kids. If it is necessary to talk to family members, be respectful. You may be working in a school that teaches kids from all kinds of backgrounds. You are not a friend. You are a teacher. Don't make the mistake of trying to get kids to call you by your first name. That takes away your power rather than adding to it because kids expect certain behavior from friends that a teacher is not able to adhere to.

Chapter 15: Recognizing Character Traits

As you become more experienced, you will instantly recognize the types of kids who are causing disruption in the class. You will also notice which kids are getting the backlash of their bad behavior. It's important that teachers start from day one recognizing the traits that kids have and knowing the kids well enough to be able to sort the class so that everyone has the best chance possible to learn. Let's look at some of the types of kids that you may come across, in order to help you to know what to do:

Belligerent Kids

These are kids who smirk at your remarks and who don't really take much notice of what you are saying. They do this in a form of bravado and have a reputation with other kids for being "cool" although that everyone won't see coolness. Get a child like this on his/her own and you will see a very different picture. These kids need their followers to help make them feel important. This can work in your advantage because when you recognize kids like this, used in a leadership position and trusting them with tasks that require their full attention, often they are very good at passing ideas to other kids within the class. It is serious lack of confidence that often makes kids like this act out. They don't have specific skills. They may have been labeled by other teachers and by society as a whole as "losers", but you can teach them to be winners by carefully picking roles for them to play. Get to know this kind of kid before trusting the child with things that may affect the morale of other students, but once you harness their ability to influence others, you really can use this to help your class to achieve.

The Shy Student

The shy student or the student who tries not to be noticed may be hiding psychological problems. Perhaps he/she hasn't learned to interact with others or has been made to feel small. Look for obvious reasons. Perhaps the child is obese. Perhaps the child is short for his age. Whatever it is that makes this child feel different to his classmates will be something you can work on. Self-esteem of a student can be seriously low if others have teased that child. Maybe the home situation is not perfect, or the family may not be able to afford the fashionable clothing that other kids are able to enjoy. Be empathetic. That doesn't mean being sympathetic. Teaching the child that he/she has value regardless of what's thought of as "cool" can help the child to see things in a better perspective. If you have group teams, make sure that this student is placed with those who will be supportive and not add to the existing problems the child may be facing.

The easy learner

Kids who learn easily without putting in too much effort can sometimes be difficult and assume themselves to be better than other students. They may act out when other kids don't get new ideas. Instead of helping to bolster their confidence, you can teach these kids all about patience. For example, if the same kid puts his hand up all the time to give you answers, don't fall for the trap of always letting him have his say. If you do this, you bolster his confidence and he already feels superior. Be honest with your marking of his work, but don't add to his ego by telling other kids they should take him as the perfect example of how a student should be.

The slow to learn

From day one, explain to the kids that you are there to help the children and that if any child doesn't get something that you have tried to explain, you are available after class to give a one to one explanation. If you do this, kids don't have to feel stupid when they leave the class with a lack of understanding of any given subject. Some teachers don't bother with this, but it really does pay off. I sat with one child for half an hour on a problem he was not able to grasp and when he grasped it, his learning skills went from strength to strength. The trouble with taking the attitude that the kids should learn from every lesson you give them, in the fundamental stages of learning, often slow kids are left behind and although you may not be the most patient of teachers, it's your teaching method that has failed if a child does not understand the basics. Every child has a different learning pace and if you can help slow kids to keep up with the class, it will make your life easier as well as the learning of the child.

Withdrawn kids

I make a special mention here of kids who seem withdrawn and are unable to mix with other kids. You need to take a little more time and actually give a little caring attention to kids like this as these kids may be suffering from psychological problems that they are finding hard to deal with. If you are really concerned about a child who is withdrawn, you can seek advice from your superiors and see what can be done to allow the child to be assessed by an educational psychologist. Often the problem is nothing to do with class. It can be a child who has suffered some kind of trauma or a child who is being abused and, as a teacher, you cannot afford to let this kind of behavior slide.

In one instance in a school where I worked, other students bullied a child and it was noted that his academic work was going downhill, and that the child was becoming very withdrawn. Because of the teacher's observation, the child was given help before attempting suicide and we later learned that the child had planned suicide. As teachers, we have a responsibility to notice when children are withdrawn and to talk to parents if we feel that this is a problem. There will also be cases where you believe a child has been hurt. These are always worth reporting. Perhaps another child has hurt the child but perhaps the area of his/her life that is causing the physical abuse is in the home.

If you notice this in your classroom, do report it to your seniors so that action can be taken to help the child. I emphasize this because in a disruptive class where you have strong kids who take the lead, you often have the kids that don't get noticed and these are the children who may have more need of help than those who draw attention to themselves all the time.

An apple for the teacher

Although it's very easy to like likeable kids, remember not to have favorites. If you do favor one child over another, you give all the wrong messages. Similarly, if something goes wrong in a class, try to avoid the old stigmatic approach of blaming all of the kids and making them all go through any kind of punishment because of the behavior of the minority. This kind of unfairness doesn't work. It makes kids dislike their peers and can cause all kinds of problems. If a punishment is given to a child for something that he/she has done, make it the same punishment as other kids get for similar offences. It is easy to forgive a child whose behavior is normally friendly although you must remember that fairness in all things is the only way to set a good example to the children you are there to teach.

If you must punish, always leave something up your sleeve because things may get worse. If you dole out punishments that are too severe, you lose power rather than gaining it because kids get the impression that they have already suffered the worst and have nothing to fear about continuing to behave in an unruly manner.

Children with Learning Difficulties and Different Attitudes

It is your job as a teacher to find out which kids are lagging behind and why. Is it because the child is a slow learner? Is the problem deeper than this? Talk to the child and try to assess what's getting in the way of his/her learning. There are also different character traits that you need to look out for but, no matter what age of children you are dealing with, you need to remember that they are children.

Maybe their home lives have not given them the best start in life that they could have had but, as a teacher, you need to treat kids with respect and help them to form their own higher self-esteem levels or to balance their esteem levels if they are overly confident but not as capable as they think they are.

The world outside is going to be a shock to all kids when they leave school and go into working life. Although you are not their parent, it's worthwhile remembering that the manner in which you deal with difficult children can make a difference to the way that they view the world. Try to find out what the weaknesses of the kids are and adjust your teaching to try and maximize their potential. Try and find out what their difficulties are with concepts relating to relationships with other kids.

If you can open up this kind of discourse, you help kids to drop bias and to work together as a team. In some instances, you may find that children have learning difficulties because of medical conditions and these kids should be treated no differently to other kids or made to feel like outsiders. Often, psychologists can help them to fit in better with their classmates.

When you work with children and see it as part of your task as a teacher to give them a more balanced view of the world, you really can make a big difference to their lives. I still remember teachers who made this kind of difference to my life and hope that, through my teaching, I have helped children to make the transition from childhood to adult with a more balanced view and losing a lot of their childhood belligerence along the way.

When teaching kids the wonders of reading, some kids don't respond well. They feel that book learning is pointless. Try getting those kids to bring in their favorite comic so that you can discuss the reading material and make reading more fun. Show kids examples where reading can be a pleasure instead of a slog. I did this with one class and got kids to come up with ideas where reading is pleasurable rather than being a negative pastime. Some of the ideas that I gleaned from involving the students turned one student from being anti-reading to actually upping his reading age. All he needed was to find the kind of reading material that made him want to learn. The rest was history.

You have to change your teaching methods to suit the kids you have each year, so don't think that a standard way of teaching works for everyone. It doesn't. Being flexible in your approach helps you to reach a larger audience and also helps you to develop your teaching skills and gives you a great deal of satisfaction when you reach one more child others considered as a failure.

The Trouble Makers

Every class has these. These are the kids who have "street credibility" and if you throw a kid out of the class, you actually empower him. He keeps that credibility and the kids know he is stronger than you. That's not a good position to be in. If you are going to assign a kid to do something because of disruptive behavior, introduce a task that is hard for the kid to do. The psychology behind this is that other kids get to see the smartarse of the class struggle. This is something that doesn't help street credibility at all. In fact, it brings that kid down to a level where he/she knows that you have the upper hand. You can ask other kids to help him/her with that task if it is too hard and by doing this, you are showing the class the strength of kids who are able to do the task easily. It helps to knock the rebellion out of a child, but you must also remember that rebellion can help you in other ways. If you get the rebellious child to want to do something, you can also bet that the others will follow. How disruptive the child is will dictate the way you play the game.

You need to find creative ways for kids to channel their energies. Kids who are disruptive may have insecurities, but when you work on these, you find that they can make great leaders. If the disruptive child is a slow learner, you can also endear the kids who learn faster to him by getting them to help him understand certain questions he has difficulty with. Remember at all times that you keep the power over the class if you don't resort to the kind of behavior that disrupted the class in the first place. For example, the following behavior should be avoided at all times:

- Violent anger toward students

- Shouting at students

- Throwing things at students

- Making students feel picked on

If you resort to any of these, you are as bad as the disruptive child and you need to look at the similarity between this kind of activity and bullying because bullying by a teacher won't work and will make your teaching less effective.

Classroom management Tips

Giving the students choices

When you find out the kid's preferences, give them choices. This means that you can take a flexible approach to their learning. Some kids will prefer to do work with you in the class, but others may be better researching and doing quizzes as homework. Encourage research and if you have the availability of a computer in the class, teach them how to research and how to find information.

Establishing goals

During the lifetime of students, they will find that goal setting helps them to achieve and to move forward in their lives. When disruption occurs, why not simply say something like "The noise level yesterday was 8. Today it's 12. Let's see if we can beat yesterday's record." Kids actually enjoy the challenge and this way, you are not nagging. You are simply setting boundaries and they are very good at using this as a form of challenge.

Having a daily schedule

You know that you have a set amount of work to do within term time and it's important to have a schedule. However, talk to your students about your schedule and let them be part of the organization of it. If you can do this, they won't blame you because you have to cover a certain number of topics within a short space of time.

Chapter 16: Utilizing Learning Activities for Classroom Management

A lot of educators will agree that the best way to teach someone is to have him actively engaged in the lesson. You can't teach someone to drive just by telling him the principles of driving. He will need to sit behind the wheel and actually drive a car in order to learn doing it. Classroom activities facilitate faster and more effective learning. They are also a very important tool in classroom management.

Teachers need to prepare good activities that the students can learn from. This will keep the students active, engaged, interested, and motivated. Giving endless lectures and letting students sit all day to memorize information are not effective ways to learn. Learning comes naturally when teachers couple information with suitable activities that the students can participate in.

Teachers should, therefore, be able to come up with good learning activities for the students. Here are some things that educators need to keep in mind when preparing classroom activities.

Qualities of Successful Learning Activities:

Clear Objective

During my teaching days, I have seen many new teachers prepare activities for their students that have no relation to their lessons. Many of their students complained later on and claimed that their money and time had been wasted. Teachers need to keep in mind that activities in the classroom should always result in learning. They can't just pick out random activities for students to do in their class hours. There should always be a clear focus and a clear learning objective for every activity done in class. Classroom activities need careful planning in order to be an effective learning tool. In addition, poorly chosen activities don't really help with classroom management and may even result in classroom problems. When students don't understand the activity and see no purpose for it, it could result to disruptive behavior. Also, when the activity has no clear focus and structure, the learners can become confused and this can hinder their learning. Therefore, in order for learning activities to be successful, they should have a specific learning objective, an evident focus, an understandable structure, and clear instructions.

Suitable for Age and Learning Level

Learning activities should be based on the students' age and level of learning. Remember that learning happens more naturally when learners are able to relate to the lesson or the activity. It can be tempting to choose activities that you think are fun or are best for your students without considering their age or learning level. However, if these activities are too advanced or too easy for them, they might not really learn from them. Or if the activity is not suitable for their age, they can become confused and will not really understand the activity. Therefore, age and learning level should be a priority consideration of teachers when formulating activities for their classes.

Safe

Learning activities must always be safe for teachers and students. Classroom activities must be approved by the school and must conform to the safety rules and regulations of the school.

Enjoyable

Teachers should make an effort to prepare classroom activities that students will not only learn from but would also enjoy. Enjoyable learning activities can have a more positive effect on the students and will ensure a better learning experience.

Modern ways of teaching incorporate fun activities in lessons to maintain students' attention and enhance the learning experience. A person can learn faster and easier when he enjoys the lesson or the activity. Moreover, the lesson is absorbed by the mind faster and the information is retained better because it is associated with a happy experience. Fortunately, teachers today are encouraged to be creative in their classes and to use as much fun learning activities as possible. Students respond better to lesson and activities that they find enjoyable so why not fill your classes with activities that they can enjoy and also learn from.

Chapter 17: Using Space Effectively for Better Classroom Management

Another essential classroom management strategy is the good use of classroom space. Every teacher needs to work with the classroom that is given her. One thing that teachers need to remember is that classroom space should be used more for the benefit of the students than the teacher. Learning should be given more priority than teaching.

Arrangement of Tables and Chairs

. Depending on the shape of the classroom and the number of students, the teacher can arrange the tables and chairs in a straight line or in a concave formation facing the board. Every teacher will need to experiment and determine the best arrangement for the student's tables and chairs in order to facilitate better learning for the students. If group activities require that tables are set in groups of four with two students facing the other two, then try that setup, too.

Classroom Size in Relation to Number of Students

One problem in public schools is the overcrowding of students in a small classroom. The school and the teachers should be able to come up with solutions for overcrowding because it can be an obstacle to effective learning. Classroom size is crucial to classroom management. When the students don't have enough space to be comfortable, it could negatively affect their ability to focus on absorbing new information. Schools and teachers should work together to make sure that students are given adequate learning space for their lessons and activities.

Seating Arrangements

Teachers usually assign seats for elementary, middle school, and high school students. This is done to prevent buddies from sitting together, resulting in chatting and noise. As a teacher, you will have to determine what kind of seating arrangement will work best to promote learning and discipline. Will you have the girls sit next to the boys, or have all girls sit on the left side and all boys on the right side? Should you allow them to choose their own seats? It's really up to you to decide which arrangement will work for each class. Don't be afraid to experiment until you find the best seating arrangement for your students.

Classroom Space and Learning Activities

It is important that you create space for your learning activities. In case classroom space is not sufficient, you can always move around the tables and chairs in order to make space or go outside your classroom and use another school facility such as the gym or the yard. Learn to use the space you have access to in order to accommodate your learning activities and don't sacrifice learning due to lack of space.

Consider Your Students' Needs

Throughout the school year, you may rearrange your classroom as often as possible in order to find the best arrangement for your students. Always be aware of your students' needs and make the necessary arrangements to help them become more comfortable and more eager to study. Shy students sometimes need help finding the right partners for group activities so that they feel they can make a contribution. You should also give special consideration to students with special needs such as those with vision and hearing problems. The same applies to students whose difficulties stem from the fact that they are learning in a second language. Be aware of all the dynamics in the classroom and, if necessary, seat students closer to the board and closer to you.

Be Flexible

Who says that learning can only happen when tables and chairs are arranged in straight lines and rows? Informal seating has become a popular practice among many teachers and if you think this can work for your class, then by all means, try it. Letting your students sit in a couch or on the ground of the school yard can be a welcome break from the usual classroom tables and chairs. This method can also be helpful when classrooms are too small for the students. Be flexible and consider alternative venues and seating for your students. Just make sure that the school approves of your methods.

Chapter 18: Managing Time Wisely

Another skill that teachers need to perfect is time management. It is a big factor that affects overall classroom management. Teachers need to make sure that lesson objectives are met and that the students are able to learn something during the class hour. When teachers have poor time management, lessons are not completed, objectives are not attained, and students are unable to learn the lesson.

Good educators understand the value of time; therefore, they know how to utilize every minute of their class so that time is not wasted. Over time, every teacher can master the skill of budgeting class time so that all parts of the lesson are completed. Perfecting class time management is not impossible. For new teachers, they might need to allot a specific time limit for each part of the lesson, writing down how many minutes should be spent on each part of the lesson and strictly timing and abiding by it. Veteran teachers will have perfected giving time limits without even looking at their timers. No matter what method you try, the bottom line is that the lesson should be completed, and the students are able to learn what you set out to teach them by the end of the class.

Nevertheless, time management does not only mean keeping the pace so that activities are completed just for the sake of completing. Students should never feel rushed so that the class can move on to the next part of the lesson. Teachers need to remember that time management should be used to optimize learning. The purpose of giving time limits to students is to help them successfully complete a certain task within a realistic, humanly possible time period. With effective time management, students can learn effectively.

One aspect of time management is progression. When teachers practice good time management in their classes, the students make cognitive progress. This is the ability to learn as they go through every step of the lesson. When classes are rushed, students move forward to the next part of the lesson without learning everything from the previous part. This creates learning gaps and leads to ineffective learning. However, when a class is well-paced and time is managed effectively, students learn all parts of the lesson, are able to connect the parts together, and become capable of understanding the lesson as a whole. This is effective learning.

The best way to ensure effective time management is to plan your lessons carefully. Create lesson plans weeks before your classes and prepare all that you will need for each lesson. Complete all the materials that you'll need for every lesson so that you won't waste precious class time looking for materials. Prepare your students' copies and anything else that they will need to use during the class. These could be photocopies, drawing materials, extra paper, coloring materials, markers, etc. Have these ready at least a day before you present your lesson to your students. Needless to say, prepare yourself by going over your lesson and studying ways to best introduce it to your students. Plan your class carefully so that time won't be wasted.

Students appreciate teachers who prepare for their classes, and they like classes that they can clearly learn from. With effective time management, students understand lessons better and learning is optimized.

Chapter 19: Promoting Good Student Behavior

One of the most effective ways to promote good student behavior is by acknowledging it and celebrating it. When good behavior is rewarded, it is repeated. And while giving punishment is needed to address poor behavior, it is not the only way to promote good student behavior in schools. Teachers should agree that good behavior is better encouraged with the use of positive methods of reinforcement, such as giving acknowledgement, recognition, or praise. By providing positive examples, students are encouraged to practice upright behavior.

Nevertheless, punishments are necessary in order to teach students that bad behavior has consequences. Because unfortunately, when bad behavior is not properly addressed, it, too, is repeated. As part of classroom management, every teacher will need to handle any improper behavior that her students show in class. For minor offenses, a teacher must exercise wisdom in handling the situation. She could give a verbal warning or just have a talk with the student. In many instances teachers have found that by inserting a comment such as, "Please refrain from talking and look this way" or "Stop tapping with that ruler", while completely staying on course, instead of giving the student undue attention, helps to diffuse the situation and discourages similar behavior in the future. Often, these methods are sufficient to solve minor behavioral problems.

Every teacher has the prerogative to her own classes and can decide what disciplinary actions to use on her unruly students. However, the disciplinary methods that she chooses for bad student behavior should always be in agreement with the school's disciplinary policies. Teachers are advised never to use methods that could negatively affect a students' physical, emotional, and mental development. Corporal punishments as well as verbal and emotional abuse in schools are all punishable by law.

Therefore, every teacher should be knowledgeable about the school's protocol on handling student behavioral problems. Teachers could send the unruly student to the guidance counselor or to the principal's office. For major offenses, the school will need to intervene and help the teacher handle the situation. The parents of the student will also be asked to help address the issue. Luckily, teachers are no longer left alone to handle student behavioral problems by themselves. With the united efforts of the teacher, the school, and the parents, a student's bad behavior can be addressed properly so that it helps the student become a better individual.

Punishing bad behavior and acknowledging good behavior are all necessary for good classroom management. Teachers will need to devise their own ways to promote good conduct among the students and to minimize the occurrence of disruptive behavior. A "Good Conduct" wall can work to acknowledge those that have good behavior. Teachers can put the names and pictures of students up there to encourage all students to be good. Giving rewards such as additional merit can also inspire students to behave in class.

Many new teachers will feel nervous when the time comes for them to discipline a misbehaving student. However, all teachers will undergo this experience. Students love to challenge their teachers in every way they can, but not all have malice in mind. Teachers will need to have lots of patience and even a sense of humor in handling naughty students.

Chapter 20: Assist & Reinforce

One way around this is to use group work or individual work to occupy the other students while you attend to the needs of those requiring more help. This can be an effective and useful strategy.

Forming the Guidelines

When you first start teaching a new class, it is fair to say that the members of that class have no idea about your expectations of them. This, of course, includes how they behave in the classroom. To sort this out, it is necessary to discuss with the class what they think correct behavior should be and any consequences that should be used if the guidelines they make are not followed. By allowing the students themselves to set behavioral and other class guidelines, they are far more likely to stick to them. These guidelines should be kept to a minimum but need to include what is expected when they are working independently, in pairs or groups.

To get the class to think about what guidelines to set, you will need to discuss with them what they find makes working easier or more difficult. Usually, the students don't need you to tell them that talking to each other while doing independent study is not beneficial for instance. The guidelines will be slightly different for pair work and group work, but you can help your students choose wisely by writing two headings on the board: Looks Like and Sounds Like. Students can then explain their guidelines by putting in detail below each heading. If the students miss a rule that, as a teacher, you know to be important, you can add it in and explain why.

Independent Work

Help your students to understand the benefits of making guidelines to follow. For independent study, they should look something like this:

- All phones and other electronic devices are to be switched off and put into the student's bag unless the teacher has specifically instructed students to use the phone for research or some other purpose for the exercise they are doing.
- No heads on desks – you need to know students are awake!
- Giving the assignment full attention.
- Putting their hand up if help is required or they have a question.
- Revising previous work once they have finished the assignment.
- Independent study should **sound** like:
- No talking in class except with the teacher, using a quiet whisper.

- Being as quiet as possible at all times. No scraping chairs or tapping pens on the table and so on.

Do a short independent study trial run and see if the students are happy with the guidelines or feel others are needed or require alteration. Over time, this may also be developed further, so check frequently with students that they are happy. Keeping them involved in the process is what makes it work and is far more effective than just setting your own set of rules they are expected to follow.

To begin with, students will "forget" a guideline from time to time, so you will need to redirect them, but they will quickly settle into the routine of how to conduct themselves during their independent study, giving you the opportunity of doing valuable one-on-one with students who need your help.

Alleviating Anxiety

Student anxiety is more common than you might expect. It generally affects older students, but primary school children are also susceptible.

The classes that cause the most anxiety are usually Math and Languages although sports and other classes can also cause problems. The anxiety can be so acute that it prevents the student from being able to think properly which can result in the problem being further exacerbated. This anxiety isn't just a student disliking the subject but can be at varying degrees including the demonstration of a full-blown phobia.

One of the first signs is avoidance of the class. If you notice students giving any excuse to leave the classroom and this happens regularly, then this is a sure sign the student is having problems.

These students will often cause disruption in the class, misbehaving or by trying to make themselves invisible by sitting at the back and keeping their heads down, so you don't notice them.

If you ask the student a question, they will become agitated, may blush and appear very self-conscious. Because the stress being caused prevents their brain from functioning normally, they find it almost impossible to think clearly and often they will not be able to answer the question.

Other signals can include:

Low or Declining Grades – Because the student finds it almost impossible to connect with the subject and their ability to absorb and process information becomes minimal, their level of achievement in the class will be low. This naturally makes the situation worse.

Crying – Students will often become so frustrated that they cry. These tears are generally to do with anger at themselves and frustration at their inability to understand.

How to Help Students with anxiety?

- Let students know that it's okay to ask for help.
- If they struggle to answer a question in class, help them out by working through it with them.
- Spend some one on one time with them to help them understand the topic.
- Praise them frequently when they get things right. Be encouraging.
- Teach them how to calm themselves by controlling their breathing.
- Let them take their time and write stuff down to help them answer the questions you have asked in class.
- Revise previous work in case an element of understanding has been missed.
- Have class conversations where you discuss negative beliefs. Reassure students that everyone learns and processes information differently. Some students will be able to pick up a concept quickly and easily while others will need more time to process it.
- Don't only use one learning technique to teach new topics. By varying the methods by which new topics are taught, you are more likely to find a connection for each student. Use learning games, EdTech, visual aids, class discussions, colorful handouts, real-life simulations, pair work, mixed ability group study, audiovisual media, and role-playing. In fact, use anything to stimulate and make the learning interesting, fun and easy to absorb.
- Ensure your students feel safe, comfortable and supported.

Know Your Students

You can learn a great deal about your students in several ways. When students are new to you, take the time to talk to them individually and learn about them. Give them a short questionnaire that asks them about themselves and has questions about:

- Their favorites type of lesson.
- Their favorite subject.
- Their hobbies or favorite activities both in and out of school.

- What difficulties they have when studying.

- What makes study easier for them?

- What helps them to focus better when studying?

- What activities do they most enjoy in class?

- What sort of activities and exercises help them to best remember the key points when learning new topics?

Note down students who are similar, so you know the types of targeted learning that is best for them. It is then possible to separate classes into groups with similar learning preferences and give them slightly more tailored work that utilizes their strengths.

Conclusion

Many approaches in this guide will work for all subjects and grade levels.

A quick reminder:

1. Be welcoming, friendly, understanding and approachable.

2. Reward good behavior rather than punishing bad.

3. Build a classroom community where students feel safe and feel like they are valued members of the group.

4. Let students create their own classroom guidelines and consequences for breaking the rules.

5. To prevent students from becoming bored, keep them busy and give them things to work on if they complete a task ahead of the rest of the class.

6. Keep work varied and interesting using different teaching techniques that can be used by students who learn in different ways.

7. Team up academically weaker students with stronger ones.

8. Keep learning based on real life so it has meaning.

9. Be understanding about possible reasons for bad behavior. Help students to recognize and address their behavior themselves.

Thank you again for purchasing this book!

I hope this book was able to help you to teach your class with confidence and deal with any classroom management issues easily and effectively. If you are a new teacher, I hope that this book can help you develop your own classroom management techniques. Don't be afraid to experiment and to try as many classroom management techniques as you think might work for your classes. Remember that teachers who practice effective classroom management strategies are able to encourage, motivate, and inspire their students to learn and to achieve.

Throughout the history of teaching, various classroom management strategies have already been developed and used. However, all teachers understand that they will need to formulate their own teaching styles and come up with their own ways to effectively handle their classes.

You now have the tools in your tool box to be effective in classroom and behavior management. Now it is time to roll up your sleeves and get your hands dirty implementing the strategies we have gone over in your classroom. You can simply use what you have learned here as it is.

Remember, teaching is a journey. A journey in which you are always reflecting, always learning, and always trying new things. My hope is that this guide will help you greatly in becoming a master at classroom and behavior management.

Thorough planning and structure will enable you to spend more time during each lesson to interact with your students and make each day enjoyable.

The next step is to put the suggestions made into practice and become an even more effective teacher.

If you enjoyed reading this book, please will you be kind enough to write a review for it on Amazon? It would be greatly appreciated! Thank you.

References

Handbook of classroom management, Emmer & Sabornie - Routledge, Taylor & Francis Group - 2015

Handbook of Classroom Management: Research, Practice, and Contemporary Issues, Carolyn Evertson-Carol Weinstein - Mahwah, New Jersey – 2006

Teachers' emotional labour, discrete emotions, and classroom management self-efficacy, Lee, Mikyoung ; Van Vlack, Stephen

The practical guide to primary classroom management, Rob Barnes 1944- ; 2006

The Culturally Responsive Classroom Management Self-Efficacy Scale

Development and Initial Validation, Siwatu, Kamau Oginga; Putman, S. Michael Starker - Glass, Tehia V.; Lewis, Chance W., Urban Education, 2017, Vol.52(7), p.862-888

https://www.edweek.org/topics/classroommanagement/index.html

https://www.scholastic.com/teachers/collections/teaching-content/classroom-management-collection-resources-teachers/

http://www.nea.org/tools/ClassroomManagement.html

http://www.ascd.org/research-a-topic/classroom-management-resources.aspx#books

https://www.commonsense.org/education/top-picks/classroom-management-apps-and-websites

https://www.edutopia.org/article/classroom-management-resources

https://globaldigitalcitizen.org/

https://www.teachthought.com/technology/14-teacher-recommended-classroom-management-apps/

https://www.educationworld.com/a_curr/archives/classroom_management.shtml

http://www.learner.org/

http://www.p21.org/storage/documents/4csposter.pdf

About the Author:

Mohamed A. Ansary is currently a lecturer of Arabic at the University of Arizona and an ACTFL-Certified OPI tester. He has been participating in programs for teaching Arabic in Egypt and abroad since 2007. In 2009 and 2010, Ansary worked at the Critical Language Scholarship Program (CLS), a program sponsored by the U.S. Department of State. In 2008 and 2009 he worked for Concordia Language Villages with high school students. From 2012-2014, he was an adjunct lecturer in the Summer SWSEEL Program in Indiana University. He also worked as an instructor for the one-year study abroad programs in Egypt for the following universities: Utah University, Montana University, London University, Leeds University, Salford University and Westminster University. He worked as a visiting lecturer of translation and English linguistics at the University of Alexandria, Faculty of Education, English Department in 2010. His area of interest in the k-16 workshops is: application of 21st century skills to the Arabic language classroom, assessment of functional abilities of Arabic language learners, using technology into the classroom, teaching culture as a fifth skill and how to integrate it into the classroom. His research interests include social media, instructional technology in the AFL classroom to increase the students' collaboration, digital literacy and intercultural competence. He is a globally connected educator. He is a passionate lifelong learner and educator. He is a global citizen. He always digs deep to enlighten his students, colleagues and himself. He synthesizes technology tools and integrate global content into his classroom instruction. He believes that culture is the fifth skill. His official website www.mohamedansary.com has been visited by instructors and learners of Arabic from 106 countries so far. Mohamed Ansary was one of the top three finalists for the Five Star Faculty Award of the academic year of 2018.

★ MENAS: https://menas.arizona.edu/user/mohamed-ansary

★ Blog: http://www.mohamedansary.com/

★ FB Profile: https://www.facebook.com/mohamedansary72

★ Instagram: https://www.instagram.com/mohamedansary72/

★ Twitter: https://twitter.com/mohamedansary72

★ Pinterest: https://www.pinterest.com/mohamedansary72/

37538251R00049

Made in the USA
San Bernardino, CA
31 May 2019